ENDORSEMENTS

WHAT PEOPLE ARE SAYING ABOUT...
JILL'S HOUSE

"Quite frankly, before I came to McLean Bible Church, I did not realize how much I had practically ignored the importance of ministry to children with special needs and their families in the church. But now, through our Access Ministry and Jill's House, my eyes have been opened to the incredible ways such ministry transforms not only the lives of these children and their families, but the life of the church. This book is an invaluable resource that will enlighten, encourage, and equip you to make God's love known to children and families that we, quite simply, must not ignore."

— **David Platt,** Pastor-Teacher,
McLean Bible Church

"Families who have kids with disabilities are often lonely and drained, like I was. But, through Jill's House families know that the leadership and staff are their partners. Jill's House is a special place where each child is honored and celebrated; and parents have a chance to catch their breath and be encouraged. At Jill's House, beauty rises from ashes, and lives are changed."

— **Carmen Jones,** Former Jill's House board member
& President of Solutions Marketing Group

"As the parents of a child with special needs, we know firsthand that rest isn't a luxury, it's a necessity. And as a couple who hopes to see the Body of Christ become a place of true belonging for the many millions of people with disabilities and their families for whom it currently is not, we can't think of a better model for ministry than Jill's House. They approach their mission strategically, their work tactically, and the families they serve with the compassion, love, and open arms that Jesus Christ commands of us. A worthy read for any church, individual, or organization seeking to extend God's love beyond its traditional borders."

— **Michael & Rebecca Lindsay,** President of Gordon College;
Ambassador for the College at Gordon College

"Jill's House is a model of Christ-like compassion for the overlooked men and women who've taken on the exhausting and overwhelming task of caring for children with special needs. In *Jill's House: The Gift of Rest,* Jill's House gives us a practical guide to respite care ministry. This is something the church and our nation desperately need."

— **Russell Moore,** President, The Ethics & Religious Liberty
Commission of the Southern Baptist Convention

"Jill's House is a beacon for our culture, signaling the way to love and empower the very ones our world marginalizes. Maybe you cannot build another Jill's House, but will you follow the way of Jesus toward those He esteems? The awe-inspiring piece of Jill's House is not found in the facility but in the extravagant love shown to families and individuals experiencing disability."

— **Matt Mooney,** Co-Founder and Executive Director
of 99 Balloons

"Jill's House: The Gift of Rest, is a comprehensive resource for those desiring to serve families who have children with developmental disabilities. This book takes you behind the scenes to demonstrate how Jill's House has achieved the gold standard in respite care. I trust the comprehensive information provided in this book will inspire and equip many to replicate the ministry of Jill's House with the incredible resources they provide."

— **Carol A. Minton-Ryan,** Professor of Sociology & Assessment Coordinator, California Baptist University

"Jill's House is without a doubt the most amazing ministry I have ever experienced. Jill's House saves families without a doubt, all members of the family: the special needs child, mom and dad, and the siblings. All need rest and restoration and all receive it in full measure. Jill's House follows what Jesus asks of us: "Feed my sheep, tend my lambs." I have been involved in disability issues for 30 years and I can tell you: Jill's House fills a need that no one else is serving. Hundreds of thousands, perhaps millions, of families in America are lost without respite. It is my prayer that every church in this great land would take the Jill's House mission to heart."

— **Steve Bartlett,** Former Mayor of Dallas, former Member of Congress & co-author of the Americans with Disabilities Act

"The impact of Jill's House on our lives has spanned both years and miles; from Vienna, VA in 2008, to Seattle, WA today! As supporters, advocates, and volunteers, we're touched by the heart, mission, vision, and overall excellence of Jill's House!"

— **Jim and Joy Zorn,** Former NFL player and head coach of the Washington Redskins; current XFL Seattle GM and Head Coach

JILL'S HOUSE

THE GIFT OF REST

JILL'S HOUSE

THE GIFT OF REST

First Edition: Year 2020
Jill's House: The Gift of Rest / Jill's House Inc.
ISBN: 978-1-946453-99-0
eBook ISBN: 978-1-951304-00-3

CHURCHLEADERS
PRESS

Colorado Springs

JILL'S HOUSE

THE GIFT OF REST

*Celebrating children with special needs, their families,
and the fullness of the body of Christ*

By
Jill's House

With
Mikal Keefer

CHURCHLEADERS
PRESS

Colorado Springs

DEDICATION

For Jill Solomon. You've been blessed by God in so many ways and you are God's blessing to so many people. Thank you for letting God use you to point people to him.

And for our Jill's House families. Thank you for letting us be a small part of your lives. It is a privilege and a joy to know you. May you all find the rest that only Jesus Christ can give.

—**Joel Dillon,** Jill's House president & CEO

CONTENTS

Section 2

FOREWORD

Before You Begin...

*M*y friends Bruce and Charlene were the perfect model of parenting a special-needs child and siblings. Their son Christopher looked just like his twin brother, Matt, with freckles, flaming red hair and a bright, beaming smile. Except, Christopher had cerebral palsy and used a wheelchair. From all appearances, having a disability in the family-mix wasn't too much for Bruce and Charlene. They displayed utter devotion to their children. They had an accessible van, were involved in their local United Cerebral Palsy chapter, and participated in church activities. Their family portrait was straight out of a politically correct ad in a *Target* circular.

Five years after I met them, I heard the shocking news that Bruce and Charlene had parted. "You must be joking," I told the bearer of bad news, "Nobody had it more together than that couple!" Apparently, I misjudged them. As did many others. Behind the scenes, Bruce had crumbled under financial stress and the pressure of Christopher's non-stop needs. He felt lost and unable to share with anyone that he was floundering. It didn't help that Charlene spent more time focusing on disability routines than on her husband. For years, their lives had run on parallel tracks and over time they grew apart. No one was more surprised about the divorce than Christopher and Matt. The situation for all involved was *heartbreaking.*

Bruce and Charlene's story is more common than you would think. One glance at statistics and you'll learn that divorce is too common among husbands and wives of special-needs children. It's why our organization, Joni and Friends, holds Family Retreats across the U.S. and in developing nations for families that include kids like Matt and Christopher. We understand the crushing 24/7 nonstop needs involved in raising children with disabilities. Our Retreats provide five days of rest, fun activities and spiritual refreshment; it's a practical, helpful response to a long-term need.

But more is required.

I thought of this the first time I visited Jill's House in McLean, Virginia shortly after its construction. I was so heartened to tour this beautiful state-of-the-art facility and meet its staff and volunteers. Everyone was dedicated to providing short-term overnight respite care for young people with intellectual disabilities. Oh, if only Bruce and Charlene had been able to take advantage of a facility like Jill's House... their family would've benefited from the sibling events, marriage counseling, Dad's nights out, and informational workshops on topics such as financial planning and school advocacy.

But not every church and community can construct and support a facility like Jill's House. And it's why I'm glad you are holding this book in your hands. Over the next few chapters of *Jill's House: The Gift of Rest*, you will learn how its vision was given birth through the remarkable story of the Solomon family. But you'll also learn how your church and community can replicate the concept behind Jill's House. You'll discover that such a vision doesn't involve a capital campaign that constructs an actual house. Rather, you will be inspired and equipped with practical tools and steps to replicate its concept of providing physical rest and spiritual renewal in Christ to needy families like Bruce and Charlene's.

Not many churches can build a facility to provide respite. But every church *can* do *something* when it comes to respite.

I encourage you to read *Jill's House: The Gift of Rest* slowly and carefully. It's filled with rich insights and practical, hands-on advice. So, grab a cup of coffee and begin turning the pages of this remarkable book—by the last chapter, you'll undoubtedly catch the vision. You'll be prepared to practice Christianity with its sleeves rolled up as it concerns lightening the load of caregivers. You'll be shaking your head and thanking God for the chance to serve.

Let's change those grim statistics about divorce. Let's lift the depression and isolation. Let's bear a bit of the burden and be like our wonderful Savior who "stands at the right hand of the needy" (Psalm 109:31, NIV). Let's help people like Bruce and Charlene, Christopher and Matt. For no one would be more pleased—or glorified—than the Lord Jesus!

—Joni Eareckson Tada
Joni and Friends International Disability Center
Agoura Hills, California

INTRODUCTION

to *Outreach's Flagship Ministries* Series

*M*aybe you've noticed: Ministry keeps you hopping. There's always one more task on your to-do list, one more email, phone call to return, one more meeting to sit through.

With so many plates to keep spinning, who has time to try something new? To pause long enough to even consider the possibilities?

Now *you* do—because the new Outreach Flagship Ministries Series connects you with best-in-class, church-rooted ministries that are shining God's love into their communities in innovative, new ways.

And these ministries aren't just doing something fresh, they're inviting you along for the ride. They've thrown open their doors to reveal not just *what* they're doing, but *how* they've made it happen.

They share the good, the bad, and "I can't believe we thought that would work" misfires that happen on the way to accomplishing something amazing.

You'll come away knowing exactly how these high-impact ministries were born, grew, and what it takes to maintain them. Plus, you'll benefit from practical advice that lets you leapfrog over pitfalls that tripped up these ministry pioneers.

This Flagship Series gives you a ringside seat to see incredible things God is doing through congregations like yours. You'll come away with doable first steps, and a roadmap for creating a best-in-class ministry of your own.

Tucked between the covers of this series you'll meet people whose faithfulness has brought about nothing less than a miracle.

And they're all about helping you bring about a miracle, too.

But this series comes with a caution: You may feel intimidated by what you see. You'll be looking at the result of years of hard work, of mistakes and midcourse corrections. It's easy to look at what a particular church or ministry has accomplished over the course of ten or twenty years, shake your head and think, "We could never pull off something like *that*."

And that would be a mistake.

We aren't suggesting you try to duplicate an existing ministry. Rather, we want to provide you with vision and inspiration of *what could be*, and practical tools to equip you *to take a next step* into something the Lord may be calling you and your church toward.

Chances are every one of the astounding ministries you'll encounter started out small. At some point it was right where you are: Someone prayerfully asking what the Lord might have them to do.

All they knew is that there was a need—and God might be calling them to help meet that need.

If you see the same need in your community, you have the same question to answer: Might God be calling you to help meet that need where you live?

We're hoping—praying, actually—that's the case.

And that you'll find your next step in meeting that need here.

— **Matt Lockhart & Mikal Keefer,**
Flagship Series Project Manager and Writer

CHAPTER 1

YOUR CHURCH AND RESPITE CARE

*C*all it the "Blue Buick" experiment.

Think about your drive to work or school yesterday. How many blue cars do you recall seeing on the road around you?

Probably none.

According to people who know, about six percent of your fellow motorists are behind the wheels of blue cars—so they're all around you. But until you're looking for them, blue cars are all but invisible.[1]

It's like that with lots of things in life: Until you're paying attention, you don't notice them. It's as if they don't exist.

What's true for blue cars is equally true of families raising children with special needs. A mom pushing a wheelchair through the park. A dad strolling along holding the hand of his daughter with Down syndrome. When's the last time you saw a scene like that?

To be fair, spotting a family raising a child with special needs can be hard to do because they aren't necessarily where you'll see them. They can't be—given the challenges of caring for a child with special needs, these families are often unable to go take in a movie, make it to the neighborhood pool, or show up at church.

They wish they could, but they can't.

And when you get a glimpse of the life they're leading, you can understand why.

The need for respite care—by the numbers

According to the National Respite Coalition, there are nearly 17 million unpaid family caregivers taking care of children with special needs in the United States.

---

1   Car Colors: https://blog.carstory.com/throwback-thursday-rare-unique-car-colors

Nearly half of those caregivers report they're overwhelmed, and that they have far more caregiving to do than they can handle. More than half spend 40 hours per week providing support to their children—and half of that number is at it 80 hours per week.

Caregiving is exhausting, emotionally draining work—and it takes a toll.

Family caregivers report suffering from physical fatigue (88%), emotional stress (81%), and experience emotional upset or guilt (81%) some or most of the time.

These are families on the edge. They're fraying and frustrated, peering into a very long, very dark tunnel without seeing even a pinprick of light at the far end.

What these family caregivers need is a break—a place they can safely leave their children for a few hours so they can rest and recharge.

Except finding those places is proving difficult.

A study done in Massachusetts echoes what's happening elsewhere in the country: Try as they might, families can't find anyone to provide respite care (64%). And even if a respite care option is located, more than half of families (52%) can't afford it.

Imagine how these families would respond if your church offered an afternoon or overnight of respite care once or twice a month.

Imagine the needs that would be met for these families.

Imagine the growth in the lives of your staff and volunteers who served.

And imagine how the character of God would be revealed to members of your congregation as families who love so deeply were drawn to find a home in your church.

The power of respite care

A study conducted by researcher Marsha Mailick Selzer found that mothers of children with autism experience a hormone associated with stress that's on par with levels found in combat soldiers.[2]

---

2   https://www.researchgate.net/publication/38068313_Maternal_Cortisol_
     Levels_and_Behavior_Problems_in_Adolescents_and_Adults_with_ASD
     https://news.wisc.edu/for-mothers-of-children-with-autism-the-caregiving-
     life-proves-stressful
     https://www.disabilityscoop.com/2009/11/10/autism-moms-stress/6121

Let that sink in for a moment.

The stress of raising an adolescent with aggressive behaviors due to autism ranks up there alongside being *shot at* by enemy troops...though there's one key difference.

Soldiers who survive combat eventually rotate off the front lines. Not so for the parents of kids with special needs. They're on the front lines forever.

Caring for their children can make sleeping through the night a distant memory. It can erode patience and empty bank accounts. It can make it next to impossible to focus on the typically-developing children in their families, the kids who've not received a special-needs diagnosis.

Because taking time for self-care feels selfish, exercise goes by the wayside. So does shopping for and cooking healthy food. More and more often dinner comes home in a sack.

Life becomes a blur of appointments with therapists, doctors, counselors, educators, and intervention specialists. There's no break, no buffer, no way to push "pause" and catch a breath.

If only there was some way these parents could rest, even for a few hours. Some way they could unwind and find respite.

There is—because your church can provide it.

Introducing Jill's House

Jill's House is a ministry that walks alongside families raising children with intellectual disabilities. Parenting any child is a blend of joy and challenges, but parenting a child with special needs often adds an additional layer of complications.

These are children who may have significant medical issues or require ongoing therapies. They might frequently require an advocate to deal with schools and insurance companies.

And the non-stop caregiving some children with special needs require can leave parents chronically sleep deprived and unable to give adequate attention to their marriages or other children.

And that's where Jill's House steps in.

Jill's House provides holistic support to every member of a family that includes a child with special needs. In addition to support groups, retreats, and other programming that will be described in this book, Jill's House offers overnight respite care.

That care was first provided in a 42,000 square-foot respite resort that sits alongside McLean Bible Church, a congregation just outside of Washington, D.C.

Parents bring their kids to Jill's House so their children can enjoy a vacation-like experience as child care specialists and volunteers love on and celebrate them.

Meanwhile, parents get a break they desperately need.

Jill's House president and CEO Joel Dillon knows how draining the challenges faced by these families can be.

Typically, these are families who can't just call a babysitter or have Grandma and Grandpa come for the weekend so they can get away to spend time together. They're giving care 24/7, and while they love their children, that constant caregiving takes a toll.

There's a high rate of divorce among these families, the typical siblings often struggle because they're not getting the attention they'd usually get, there's financial stress...if my family were in the same situation, it would take a toll on us, too.

Respite is what they say is most needed for the health of their families. And respite is something almost no one is providing.

So, Jill's House stepped in and said, 'We'll do it.' And we've seen families respond to our offer of rest in amazing ways.

What sets Jill's House apart from nearly all other respite care facilities is that it provides overnight care for children.

"Parents send us their kids for 24 to 48 hours several times throughout the year, and we give them a great experience," said Joel. "Our facility was tailor-made for these kids—it's like a Disney World experience for them."

We know, we know—your church doesn't have anywhere near McLean Bible Church's membership and resources. But you don't need to build another Jill's House to bring respite care to your community. You likely already have pretty much everything you need to launch a respite care ministry—*if* you're willing.

Just start small, and see what happens.

Jill's House can trace its beginnings to four children with disabilities meeting in a Sunday school classroom while their parents enjoyed an hour's respite in church.

You can do that—and if that's as big as your respite ministry ever gets, you'll still have a massive impact in the lives of four families. You'll make it possible for them to carve out precious hours for rest and spiritual renewal, to glance up from challenges to see one another, and Jesus, more clearly.

But those families aren't the only ones who'll benefit.

Equally impacted will be you and your church.

As you open up your building for respite care, you're opening your hearts to loving people who reflect the image of God. People who are gifted and called to ministry, and who will enrich your congregation in powerful ways.

And because you'll decide how many children you can care for and what types of needs you're equipped to accommodate, you can scale a respite care ministry to your facility and the skills of your staff or volunteer team.

Jill's House went big with overnight, weekend-long care—and you can do that, too. Or you can do what they did for years before building a facility: Host an afternoon of respite care on Saturdays. Give families a break on Friday evenings. Host family events at a nearby campground.

If respite care is something for you, of course.

If it's something that God might be calling you to try.

Which—probably no surprise here—we think God might very well be doing.

The biblical case for special needs and respite care ministries

God has called you to be a good steward of your congregation's resources, and if your church is like most, there never seem to be quite enough resources to do everything you think you should be doing.

So perhaps you're wondering about the biblical basis for your church launching a special needs or respite care ministry. With so many ministries to fund and maintain, why put special needs and respite on the list?

The Bible makes it clear missions are a must—Jesus himself told his followers to spread the word.

Caring for widows and orphans is also a priority. The Bible spells that out clearly. Ditto for worship, teaching, and preaching.

And since Jesus waved children past his disciples so he could bless them, children's ministry must be close to his heart, too.

But serving families raising children with special needs?

In the Bible, you don't see Jesus intentionally gathering together people who seem to have intellectual disabilities. He doesn't deputize his disciples to go provide respite care for their families.

So, with everything else to do, is creating special needs and respite care ministries something that's equally important...or just a nice thing to do if there's extra time and money?

Consider....

- **You're called to reach out to people in your neighborhood, too** (Acts 1:8).

"One thing most people don't know about parents who are raising kids with special needs is that they're essentially an unreached people group," said Joel. "In our experience, the vast majority of these families are outside the church, cut off from the Body of Christ. Like all of us, they're desperately in need of the Gospel of Jesus Christ.

That's why it's so important that Jill's House sees them and reaches out to them and that the church does as well."

Jill's House provides a tangible service to families: overnight respite care for their children so parents get a break from the everyday grind of caring for their kids.

But that's not all Jill's House does.

"We boldly proclaim the Gospel to these families and do everything in our power to love them towards Jesus Christ," said Joel. "And by God's grace, I think at we've been able to do both of those things in great quantity and quality over the years."

Your church's special needs and respite care ministries will break down barriers keeping families raising children with special needs away from experiencing community with the church—your church.

When Shannon and Matt, a couple raising two children with special needs, were seeking a church home, they found themselves checking out congregations with one question foremost in mind: Would the congregation have anything to offer to their children?

When they rolled their daughter's wheelchair into the vestibule of a small Anglican church, they noticed someone quickly approaching from across the lobby.

It was the children's pastor who, after pausing to smile at little Waverly, straightened up and said words that took Shannon's breath away.

"I have no idea how to care for your children," the pastor said, "But I'm willing to learn if you'll teach me."

"It was an amazing moment," remembers Shannon.

Their family had just found their new home.

- **All people are created in God's image** (Genesis 1:26)

There's no prescribed set of characteristics that defines what someone created in God's image looks like. Each person is unique.

And, suggests Joel Dillon, God was intentional about shaping each and every person.

> *Many of the children we serve will never have a job. They'll never get married, perhaps never walk or talk, and their life expectancies may be shorter than most other people. So, some look at these children and feel pity, or decide they're somehow "less than."*
>
> *But when you're in contact with children with disabilities and their families daily like we are at Jill's House, you see that God was not asleep at the wheel when he created these children.*
>
> *He created them in his image and that image is going nowhere. We're here to love and serve them in every way we possibly can and to recognize them as image-bearers."*

When your church embraces children with special needs and sees them clearly—as God's creations reflecting his majesty, glory, and character—something shifts in your church culture.

You begin experiencing acceptance and a welcoming spirit more broadly. Your congregation begins looking outward rather than inward, sharing with others the love that God has given you.

When you celebrate the dignity of some of God's creations, it's easier to celebrate the dignity of all of them.

- **All people are gifted by God** (1 Corinthians 12:4)

God has gifted every believer with a way to honor him and bless others. And people living with disabilities are no exception.

"God has given the children we serve gifts he wants them to share with the body of Christ," said Joel. "At Jill's House, we have the opportunity to see those gifts and what God is doing in and through their lives. I just wish more people could see and experience that."

They can—and you will—as you welcome children with special needs and their families into your congregation.

Some people with disabilities have already been welcomed and are blessing the church in remarkable ways:

Joni Eareckson Tada is penning bestsellers and leading an international ministry following an accident that left her a quadriplegic.

Rick Warren filled the pulpit at Saddleback Church in Southern California, even though a brain disorder caused him to experience dizziness, temporary blindness, and confusion when his body produces adrenaline.

Billy Graham didn't see his diagnosis of Parkinson's disease as a mandate to retire from his calling to evangelize, though he was clearly impacted by his disease.

Amy, a 13-year-old member of the Jill's House program who has Down syndrome, regularly serves in her church by distributing bulletins to the people she greets as they enter the sanctuary.

And then there are all the people already filling your pews.

Elderly people who can no longer navigate stairs. Veterans who returned from serving their country with physical limitations or PTSD. Congregants coping with depression, A.D.D., or dyslexia.

God's given them all gifts, and they're the very people serving in your ministries. You need their gifts to be a fully formed body, to participate in God's mission in your community.

Imagine what God will be able to do when you've invited an entirely new group of families and their gifts into your family.

- **And those gifts are *needed* in the Body of Christ**
  (1 Corinthians 12:7)

  "I think it's important not just to include people with disabilities, but to create a culture of belonging," said Joel. "It's not enough to just say, 'Yes, you can come here and worship with us on Sunday mornings.' We also need to find places for people to use their gifts, whether it's in volunteering or serving in another way."

  Visit McLean Bible Church, and you'll see people with disabilities visibly serving throughout the many ministries of the church.

  But don't be mistaken: They're not serving to give them something to do. They're serving because they're *needed* in those ministries. They bring gifts and skills and passion and purpose that make those ministries function.

  "The church needs to find opportunities for people with disabilities to use their gifts," Joel said, "Just like we'd do for anyone else."

- **And God calls *all* people to become his friends** (Matthew 11:28; Romans 5:8)

  A disability—physical, intellectual, or otherwise—in no way precludes someone from being loved and desired by God.

  There are not second-class citizens or plus-ones in the Kingdom of God.

  We're all specifically, individually invited to become part of what God's doing.

  "There are very few people coming to McLean Bible Church who've not been blessed by a family raising a child with disabilities," said Joel. "When a church finally opens its eyes to these families and the gifts they bring, that's when that congregation becomes passionate about special needs and respite ministry."

  Who is God calling you to invite into your community of faith? Whose gifts are sitting on the sideline, idling, waiting for you to notice?

  And what might the impact be if your current church members used their gifts to launch a ministry of providing respite to families who could use it?

  Tricia and Dick Schmehl know the answer to that question.

Katie Schmehl was 13 months old when her parents, Tricia and Dick, discovered their daughter had been born with agenesis of the corpus callosum.

"She was missing tissue that allows the left side of the brain to communicate with the right side," explained Tricia. "There are lots of adults walking around who have a partial corpus callosum and they're fine. You can be missing up to about 40 percent and function well. But Katie has a near complete absence of the tissue and that causes significant global delays."

Katie is non-verbal, has balance issues, and lives with some challenges.

"She's sweet, with a genuine smile, and she loves people," said Tricia, "But she can't be left alone. She can't control her behavior, and as she grew older and got frustrated with not being able to communicate, it became clear we couldn't control her behavior, either."

Add to the list of Katie's issues that she found it impossible to sleep through the night, and Tricia and Dick were on a collision course with an unsustainable life.

The Schmehls connected with Jill's House during Katie's teenage years. Katie was one of the first children who stayed at Jill's House, and Tricia said it changed their family's life.

"Dick and I were like two ships passing in the night," she said. "We were both sleepless and frustrated. And when you're in survival mode, you're at your worst as an individual and can't participate in your marriage."

Tricia said she and Dick were on the path to separation when the opportunity to participate in respite care appeared.

It was a game changer.

"All we did on the weekends Katie was at Jill's House was sleep," she said. But sleep is exactly what the couple needed.

"We credit Jill's House with keeping us together," Tricia said. "There was no way for us to come together as a couple until Jill's House came into the picture."

Respite care may well be a ministry God is calling you to consider. And your friends from Jill's House have good news and even better news for you.

First the good news: Embracing a respite care ministry will bless more than your community. Your church will be touched, shaped, softened, and encouraged in ways you never thought possible as you step into providing this service.

And here's the even better news: This *is* something you can do. You don't need to be a mega-church. You don't have to have a newly-built facility.

You can do this.

And your church will be richer for it.

CHAPTER 2

THE BIRTH OF JILL'S HOUSE

*E*very church ministry has a start—the birth of Jill's House began with the birth of one particular child: Jill Solomon.

Jill was a beautiful, healthy baby but also something of a surprise.

"Life was really good for our family," said Brenda Solomon, Jill's mother. "My husband, Lon, was the senior pastor of McLean Bible Church, and between the church and raising our three boys, we stayed plenty busy."

But then, at nearly 40, Brenda discovered she was once again pregnant.

"I could hardly believe it, but we embraced the blessing. We figured we'd just take the baby with us wherever we went. She'd be on the sidelines at the boys' baseball and soccer games, and we'd bring the baby to their school events," she said. "Plus, it was icing on the cake when we discovered this new baby would be a girl."

The pregnancy was routine, and Jill's delivery went without any complications. Lon and Brenda headed home from the hospital carrying the sweetest little girl either of them had ever seen.

"From the moment we took Jill home she was the family princess," Brenda remembers. "We were delighted and the boys were amazing. Our 7-year-old was so tender—every day he'd say, 'Jill, you're beautiful and I love you.' And then the bottom fell out."

Embracing the new normal

When Jill was nearly three months old, Brenda noticed something unusual while changing Jill's diaper.

"Her hand was shaking," said Brenda, who pointed it out to Lon.

Lon just shrugged. "She's our fourth baby and babies do strange things," he said. And Brenda—veteran mom of three active boys—couldn't disagree. She didn't give it another thought.

That was on a Tuesday. By Saturday, Brenda was thinking about little else.

"Lon was putting finishing touches on a sermon when I saw Jill doing it again, but this time it was the other side of her body shaking."

Brenda and Lon grabbed a video camera to record the seizure, and when they visited their doctor several days later for Jill's immunizations, they took the film along.

The doctor watched it carefully—several times. Then he paused before gently saying, "I think those are focal seizures."

Neither Brenda or Lon had ever heard of focal seizures, but they figured some medication would be required, maybe a visit to a neurologist, and then Jill could move on seizure free.

They were wrong.

In spite of everyone's best efforts, Jill's seizures not only continued, they worsened. At first, they gripped just half of Jill's tiny body, but within a few more months, she was experiencing life-threatening grand mal seizures.

"The seizures just wouldn't stop," remembers Brenda, "And they turned our family upside down. I can't begin to explain how sad and afraid we felt. Everything in our family went on hold as we tried to save our daughter's life."

Caring for Jill became a full-time job for Lon and Brenda—more than full-time. Because Jill experienced seizures throughout the day and night, either Lon or Brenda had to be fully focused on her at all times.

Their lives became a blur of frantic 911 calls. Ambulance runs to emergency rooms. Consultations and medicine regimens that seemed to accomplish nothing. Extended hospital stays.

And more than once they knelt over Jill, praying as they frantically did their best to care for her as the howl of distant sirens grew closer.

Plans were constantly cancelled, vacations impossible. Their sons' school and sports events were missed.

And everyone—Brenda, Lon, and Jill's brothers—were helpless to fix what was broken, as together they watched Jill seize time after time after time.

"When you start on a journey like this, you're strong," said Brenda. "You're emotionally and physically healthy, but that doesn't last long. Then whatever reserves you have are gone and worn away. You're exhausted and your only goal becomes to make it through one more day, to last one more hour. And you can't see how you or your family can possibly go on."

Life began unraveling for Brenda and Lon. There was simply no time for self-care, no energy for thinking about the future. In spite of their supportive marriage and solid Christian faith, they felt increasingly isolated and alone.

As she struggled through those trying days Brenda said God gave her a verse from the Bible to cling to:

Don't be afraid, for I am with you. Don't be discouraged, for I am your God. I will strengthen you and help you. I will hold you up with my victorious right hand. (Isaiah 41:10 NLT)

"That verse became my anchor," said Brenda, who repeated and prayed it often.

But even as Brenda clung to the truth of that passage, she couldn't take her eyes off Jill who, despite Johns Hopkins physicians, continued to be wracked by seizures.

There was still no diagnosis. Still no treatment plan promising anything more than trying yet another cocktail of medication. Still no hope for flipping whatever switch in Jill's brain caused her to lose consciousness, convulsing as she swayed at the edge of a stroke, or worse.

And at Jill's side, day and night, week after week, stood Brenda and Lon.

Brenda and Lon, who were beyond exhausted.

Brenda and Lon, who hadn't had a full night's sleep since what felt like forever.

"When Jill was two and a half years old, a day came when the boys were at school and Lon had left for the office," said Brenda. "I was where I always was, beside Jill as my little girl lay on the floor seizing. It felt as if I was finally being swept down into a bottomless pit. Emotionally, physically, spiritually, I had nothing left to give. In my devastation I cried out to God. I said, 'She's yours. Step in and do something. The only thing I ask is that you use her life. Don't waste this pain—use it for your glory."

Brenda paused, collected herself, and then continued.

"That's the day I got a phone call from a woman I'd never met."

That call became a lifeline—one that sparked what would years later become Jill's House.

The power of respite

The woman at the other end of the phone call was Mary Doremus.

Mary was attending McLean Bible Church, but Brenda had never met her. The truth was Brenda hadn't gone to church for months. She couldn't—it would have meant leaving Jill and risking Jill's life.

"To be honest, I'm not sure how Mary got my number," said Brenda. "But she told me she wanted to come over to meet Jill and me. We arranged a time and she stopped by. Mary sized up our situation quickly and told us she wanted to gather a group of people to pray for our family. All she asked is that we write a prayer letter each month—that we give them an idea of what we wanted them to pray about. I didn't have energy to do much, but I knew I could do that."

Mary wouldn't tell Brenda and Lon who was in the group—that's something that decades later they still don't know.

But not only did the group pray, they also banded together to fund a part-time caregiver who showed up to be with Jill so Brenda and Lon could get respite—and a full night's sleep.

"It totally changed our lives," marvels Brenda.

Having a caregiver occasionally take a shift watching Jill didn't change Jill's health; she continued to get worse, not better.

But the opportunity to rest—to relax and be refreshed—lifted the exhaustion that was dragging Brenda and Lon downward. It let them be with their boys and one another and allowed them to see beyond the immediate demands of Jill's health crisis.

"It was naïve, but we'd thought we could just tough it out," said Lon. "It had never occurred to us to ask for help. But once we experienced respite, we could see a bit of light at the other end of the tunnel."

Brenda and Lon both realized that if respite care could make such a difference in their family's life, perhaps it could have the same impact in the lives of other families who were in similar situations.

"When I realized how much we'd needed this," Brenda recalls. "I began to wonder how we could give this gift to other families living with children with special needs."

That was the moment the Solomons first felt a burden to help families who didn't have a Mary in their lives. And as a pastor who values outreach,

Lon quickly realized that a respite care ministry could deepen the church's involvement in the lives of their community.

"We thought respite could even be an outreach of our church, and a way of sharing the love of Christ with families and their children," said Lon.

The more Lon and Brenda talked about the idea, the more excited they became. McLean Bible Church could provide help to families no matter what the families believed. Respite care was so scarce and the impact so great, families that might not be open to a church would welcome respite care, even if a church was offering it.

"Maybe once they realized we were coming alongside their families because we authentically cared, they'd be open to why we cared," said Lon, who felt that even if no family ever came to faith or joined McLean Bible Church, serving families with special needs children was something God was calling McLean Bible Church to do.

"Think who Jesus hung out with when he was here on Earth," Lon said. "He was with special needs people all the time. Deaf people, blind people, sick people like lepers, even *dead* people—and being dead is a *major* disability. We realized that these children and their parents were very close to the heart of Jesus. And we also realized that if we served them and they didn't come to Christ that wasn't a failure. It would be a sadness for us, yes, but not a failure. We'd have been faithful serving in the name of Jesus and that's never a failure."

So Lon and Brenda accepted a burden they felt God gave them and started praying and planning. Something had to be done, but what? How do you go about providing respite care to an entire community?

"Do you hire an army of nannies and send them into people's homes?" said Lon. "Where do you come up with the money for that? Do you set up an endowment? We had absolutely no idea where to start."

But it seems God already had that covered.

He'd already begun moving in the heart of Diane Anderson.

CHAPTER 3

THE ARRIVAL OF ACCESS MINISTRY

"*W*hen my husband and I started attending McLean Bible Church, we saw a notice in the bulletin," said Diane. "It said a couple was looking for a volunteer to walk the halls with their non-verbal 7-year-old son so the parents could attend church."

Diane had never seen an announcement like that in a church bulletin, but since McLean had two morning services, it wouldn't take much to hike during one and worship during the other.

Diane pointed out the notice to her husband. "I said, 'Well, we could do that.'"

On long loops through the church hallways, Diane got to know both the little boy and his parents. And then, sitting in the worship services, she began to notice there were other parents with special needs children who could use help.

One mother hovered at the back of the sanctuary keeping an eye on her socially-anxious daughter, who sat at a card table in a side room doing puzzles.

Two boys with autism were tucked away in a private classroom with a volunteer who was doing her best to engage and teach them. None of the existing Sunday school classes were properly equipped to welcome these boys into their class.

Given the size of McLean Bible Church, Diane was sure there were other children with special needs who were hidden around the peripheries of the congregation. Either that or their families simply didn't come to church because they didn't feel welcome once they arrived.

What these children and their parents needed, Diane decided, was access.

Access to the gospel. Access to acceptance. Access to friendships with other children.

Plus, their parents needed access to a worship service—something that was difficult while caring for their kids with special needs. But what if there was a class for these children? That would free up their parents for a precious hour of fellowship, worship, teaching, and prayer.

So, Diane approached the pastor, Lon, to ask about finding space for a class. Someplace that children with special needs would be welcome while parents headed down the hall to the church sanctuary for an hour of respite.

"At that time, I didn't know Lon had a child with special needs. I hadn't heard about Jill or seen her, because she didn't come to church." said Diane. "Lon was receptive—very receptive. He knew the need and quickly gave his ok."

It's worth pausing at this point to mention that Diane sailed over what can be a hurdle for many people who want to launch a special needs or respite ministry: She got an immediate approval to give it a try.

If you're looking to start or expand a respite ministry, you'll probably have to go through an approval process—one that will move more smoothly if you take advantage of the advice beginning in Chapter 11.

But that's down the road. For now, let's rejoin Diane.

Humble beginnings

Diane cleaned out an unused room and set up a little classroom for the four kids with special needs she knew about in the congregation. She issued a personal invitation and the next week all four showed up.

The following Sunday all four came back—and they weren't alone. Now Diane had *eight* children in her class, and as the weeks went by the number kept growing.

Clearly, she needed a bigger room.

"It all took off from there," said Diane. "Each week we seemed to have more children show up."

Attendance grew as Diane encouraged parents of students to spread the word, and she reached out to the special needs community. The newly named "Access Ministry" was thriving...but there was a problem.

"Lon feared that this ministry might be viewed as self-serving," said Diane. "Given that his daughter has special needs, might this be viewed as all about Jill? We were serving lots of kids, but we didn't want it to become an issue."

The solution was that Diane had to raise any money needed to fund Access from sources outside the church budget. Fortunately, she didn't find that difficult—several families provided what was needed as the ministry continued to grow.

"Eventually, I went to the church board and they approved Access as a funded ministry of the church," said Diane. And Diane, who was a part-time staff member in the preschool area while volunteering time to Access, was brought on to direct the special needs ministry.

She acknowledges that she was an unlikely choice.

"I was a travel agent," laughed Diane. "On paper there was nothing that suggested I could or should be the person to guide a special needs ministry. But Lon knew my heart, and I was selected."

She proved to be a great hire. Diane not only knew what it took to provide care for children, she understood intimately the difficulties families with special needs kids faced as they coped with life—and attending church.

"My son, Christopher, was diagnosed with Asperger's Syndrome," said Diane. "At Sunday school, he wouldn't join the circle time and that didn't work for his teacher—who eventually told me he wanted Christopher out of his class. I pointed out that Christopher was listening, that he *was* paying attention. It's just that Christopher couldn't do it while sitting in a circle. Christopher could do it while sitting under a table."

Diane offered to provide training so the teacher would better understand how to work with a child with special needs like Christopher, but the teacher wouldn't budge on his expectation. Christopher needed to get out from under the table and into the circle...or go elsewhere.

So, a different teacher—one who'd worked with Christopher in the past—stepped into the classroom.

"She found ways to include Christopher, even though my son was hunkered under the table," said Diane. "If the story was about Jonah, guess who was in the belly of the whale? If they were talking about Daniel, it was Christopher in the lions' den. She adapted how she presented stories so he had a part."

And because Christopher was often cast in a starring role, other kids would join him under the table. "He loved that," said Diane.

Eventually, Christopher found his way out from under the furniture to join the other children. He's now grown, married, has kids of his own, and works as a nurse. He's living with Asperger's and succeeding in life, though he still remembers that teacher who wanted to boot him out of Sunday school.

Even more, he remembers the teacher who chose to include him.

What *Diane* remembers is the church—her church—embracing her son and giving her the freedom to participate in worship services and also serve other children and their families.

"When we care for kids with special needs we're caring for their parents," said Diane. "We're providing respite care, even if it's only for an hour or two."

Diane left Access after a dozen years to stay home with her growing children, but remains active in the special needs community. She volunteers at Jill's House and sits on the boards of Arc and the local branch of the Autism Society—organizations that promote and protect the human rights of people with intellectual and developmental disabilities.

All five of her kids, who are now grown, are serving people with disabilities.

"My life verse in the Bible is 1 Samuel 16:7," said Diane. "It tells us that while people look at outward appearance, the Lord looks at the heart. When I look at someone with autism, down syndrome, or cerebral palsy I see a gift from God. I've spent a lifetime getting to know the most beautiful hearts in the most amazing people. Some of those people I've never had a conversation with—they aren't verbal—but I've seen their hearts and they are beautiful beyond words."

A shift in culture

When Access became a part of McLean Bible Church, it didn't impact just one or two rooms at the far end of the Christian Education wing.

Access pulled special needs families further into the orbit of the church and, as a result, McLean's culture shifted. What had been essentially a culture of benign neglect regarding special needs became one of inclusion— and more importantly, belonging.

To be clear: Nobody at the church was actively shunning or ignoring families of children with special needs. Had you asked, you'd have been told the church valued children—all children. Embraced families—all families. Wanted to reach people with the Gospel—all people.

If you'd asked, you'd have been told all were welcome at McLean Bible Church, and the people who said that meant every word. They were kind, caring people, eager to share the gospel and embrace all who came.

They had a heart for service, one that was expressed in countless ways. Except...

When you're the parent of a special needs child you know when you're not really included. You know because you've encountered so many situations where your child might be tolerated, but he or she isn't fully welcome.

You've learned to count the glances and stares, to notice whether someone has thought to make navigating a wheelchair through aisles easy or difficult. You take note of the toileting options, the van-friendly parking, the convenience of getting in and out of the building, and of who smiles, and who looks away in discomfort.

And if the right accommodations aren't evident, you know your child wasn't invited to this particular party. Whether or not the message is intentional, you receive it loud and clear: Nobody has thought to make it easy for your child to be there.

When Access Ministry was launched in 1996, McLean Bible Church trumpeted a very different message: Special needs children *were* welcome— as were their parents. The church was a safe, supportive place for families facing the challenges that special needs bring. They'd be greeted with sincere enthusiasm.

It meant that, in the youth group, siblings of special needs kids would be safe talking about what life is like when your parents are so overwhelmed by caring for a brother or sister that you survive on leftover attention.

It meant that when a child occasionally called out and his voice echoed through the sanctuary, it would be received less as an interruption and more as a joyful noise that blessed not just God but also the entire congregation.

It meant the congregation was looking *toward* people with special needs, not *around* them.

As the culture of the church moved to intentional inclusion, more and more special needs families made the drive into northern Virginia to attend services.

And the congregation found more and more ways to signal that those families weren't just welcome, they were cherished. McLean championed the dignity and value of those with disabilities.

The church turned the corner to becoming an advocate for people with special needs, living out a belief that they're full members of the body of Christ, people with something to contribute.

But while inclusion was good and advocacy better, the church still wasn't addressing the burden Lon and Brenda Solomon felt kicking around inside them. They still wanted to provide respite care that lasted longer than just during Sunday services.

They'd prayed about it, talked about it, and tossed around ideas, but nothing much was happening.

"Then, when Jill was four, Lon and I went to an early intervention meeting at a public school she'd be attending," remembers Brenda.

Other parents with special needs children were there too and, as the Solomons made their way to their car following the meeting, Lon commented about how tired those other parents looked.

"Lon was going on and on," Brenda said. "So, I said to him, 'If you're so concerned, why doesn't McLean Bible Church finally *do* something about it?'"

That elbow-in-the-ribs question was something Lon couldn't shake.

Why *didn't* the church do something about it? But what exactly *could* the church—as large and influential as McLean Bible Church was—actually do?

Jill had opened the Solomons' eyes to the need for a special needs ministry, but was it possible to do more? Was there a way that the church could offer respite care, too?

The answer, of course, was "yes..." And Diane Anderson thought she knew how.

Access extended

Diane was scarcely keeping up with the growth of the Sunday morning program, when she found herself waking up at night wondering what else she could do to provide respite to families.

"We knew there were families out there who wouldn't send their kids to a Sunday School class," said Diane. "They weren't up for attending church either, but they'd sign up for respite care."

Within a year, Diane launched "Break Away," a respite program that provided care between 10:00 a.m. and 3:00 p.m. one Saturday per month.

"We took children with disabilities and also their typical siblings," said Diane. It was essential to provide programming for both so parents could, if they chose, have no parenting responsibilities for a few precious hours.

The church hired a nurse to handle seizures, feeding tubes, and whatever other medical needs arose. Volunteers buddied up with children, and the program charged $15 per child to cover costs.

When the program went live, parents lined up to participate. What were monthly sessions quickly became weekly events.

McLean still wasn't providing the in-home respite care the Solomons found so helpful, but Diane didn't see how the church could make that work. State and Federal regulations would have hamstrung any efforts she made to arrange extended in-home care, and she lacked the bandwidth to fight those battles.

"We couldn't pull it off," said Diane, "But I was careful to pair up visiting families with specific volunteers. The consistency helped friendships develop. When I mentioned that a visiting family might benefit from occasional in-home help, it was often offered by volunteers who'd become their friends."

Since that in-home care wasn't an official Break Away service, just friends helping friends, the rules and regulations didn't apply and families still got the help they needed.

"And it was a great way to have the Gospel walk into someone's house," said Diane.

As you dive into the details of sorting out your respite program, do what Diane did: Keep first things first. Your goal is to share God's love through respite care, not to just provide respite care.

It may seem to be a small difference, but it impacts everything.

It's the difference in what motivates your volunteers. It sharpens the focus of your programming and determines whether you approach your respite care ministry prayerfully or just pragmatically.

Diane bathed all significant decisions concerning Access in prayer. And God showed up, week after week.

"We saw families come to faith in God all the time," said Diane. "Some parents would arrive at our respite program the first time and say, 'I'm not religious and I don't want my kid hearing about Jesus.' I'd have to tell those parents, 'Well, I'll be honest: We talk about Jesus here.' Almost always a reluctant parent would think that over and then say, 'Well, fine. Go ahead.' Those parents needed the care more than they needed to protect their kids from hearing about Jesus."

Diane found it fun watching God work in the lives of visiting families.

"They were desperate for a hope they didn't know they needed until they walked through our door. In time, they'd tell us how hopeless and lost they felt, and then how they couldn't understand why we'd welcome and celebrate their children," Diane said. "I'd tell them, 'That's easy: God tells us to love our neighbors and you're our neighbors.'"

It might take weeks or even months, but Diane saw reluctant parents' hearts soften. McLean Bible Church's respite care programs became a powerful outreach for sharing the Gospel.

Which is one reason that, a few months after offering a Saturday respite time, Diane launched "Break Out," a Friday evening program.

Parents could drop off kids at 6:30 p.m. and had until 10:00 p.m. to return and pick them up. Like the Saturday program, children with special needs were treated to a fun time of music, movies, games, snacks, crafts, and love in Jesus' name.

And like Saturday's Break Away, Friday night's Break Out quickly became a weekly event. Even then, families were limited to one visit per month because the waitlist was so long.

Both respite programs continue to serve real needs and shine a light into the Northern Virginia region.

But still—what about providing overnight respite care? The kind that would allow parents to get a full night's sleep or even slip away for a weekend?

The Solomons searched for someone, anyone, who was providing that level of care and came up blank. The Access team was also on the lookout, with the same results.

And then, a trip to Israel changed everything.

CHAPTER 4

SHALVA—A MODEL OF CARING

*L*on Solomon had gotten in the routine of leading an annual tour to Israel. The tours were pretty much what you're picturing: busy days bouncing between key biblical sites, punctuated by Lon's Bible studies and teaching.

Anyone leading an international tour knows there's no end of details to arrange, no shortage of balls to juggle, and expectations to meet.

When someone asked Lon to put the tour on hold long enough to check out a Jerusalem-based program called "Shalva," Lon couldn't think of something he wanted to do less.

"I didn't have five minutes to spare, let alone an hour for a tour," remembers Lon. But when Lon heard the story behind Shalva, he made time.

Shalva's founders, Malki and Kalman Samuels, had founded the center after their young son, Yossi, became blind, deaf, and acutely hyperactive. Their story of exhaustion and isolation sounded familiar to Lon, as did their deep desire to do something to help their son.

When well-intentioned friends suggested institutionalizing Yossi, Malki made a vow to God: If he'd help Yossi, she'd give herself to helping other children with disabilities and their families.

When Yossi turned 8 years old, that breakthrough came in the form of a special education teacher who found a way to forge a connection with Yossi. Once Yossi discovered that the word *"schulchan"*—which is Hebrew for table—referred to that piece of furniture in the Samuels' kitchen, other words quickly followed.

Malki remembered her promise to God, and she and Kalman founded Shalva[3] in 1990.

---

3   https://www.shalva.org/about-shalva-2

At first, Shalva was an afternoon playgroup for children with special needs. Gradually, the program expanded to support a broader range of special needs and a broader range of ages, from birth through adulthood.

Nine years after Shalva launched, Lon found himself standing in what he'd thought didn't exist: the lobby of a facility providing overnight respite care.

He immediately phoned Brenda with the news: He'd finally found it. He'd found a model for the kind of place they'd dreamed of creating. It was possible after all—and now they had an example of how it could look in real life.

Having that model was essential in moving the dream of a Jill's House closer to reality.

"Most people can't jump from a concept to building something," said Lon. "But if there's a working model they can see, then they can get on board. Shalva became that model for Jill's House, a working example of what Jill's House could be."

A few years after Lon first visited, Brenda went to Shalva as well—and took a team of five with her.

The team met with staff, videotaped the facility, and studied the procedures involved in running a respite center. Additional teams from McLean Bible Church followed to receive training from Shalva leaders and caregivers.

Don't brush past Lon's insight that a working model is important if you want to launch something new—including a respite ministry. You'll experience far more success and get far more support when you don't just *tell* leaders in your church about respite care, but you *show* them as well. This is where Jill's House can help.

Do your homework (we suggest some organizations to contact in Chapter 24) to find a church near you engaged in providing some level of respite care. Take your leaders on a field trip to see it in action.

You'll be stunned how open other ministries will be with you offering insights and information. You're not competitors; you're fellow servants.

McLean Bible Church and later, Jill's House, followed the trajectory of starting small, finding a mentor, and gradually moving into a larger, more involved ministry.

Now, 30 years after Shalva's first playgroup met, the Shalva National Center is a resource for therapy, education, and recreation to hundreds of individuals with special needs. It also provides respite, advocacy, and family support, and its programs have been so successful that the Jerusalem Municipality provided the organization a site near the Jerusalem's Shaare Zedek Medical Center.

The focus of Jill's House is on respite, but having the advice of an older, more experienced organization is a huge plus—and one that helped launch Jill's House.

Establishing your respite care ministry isn't something you have to do alone. In fact, you *shouldn't* do it alone if you have the opportunity to team up with other churches in your community.

At minimum, make contact and find out what they're doing and when they're providing care. That information will help you know how to shape your ministry.

CHAPTER 5

THE BUILDING OF A DREAM

A vision for serving God and the community?
Check.
A ministry that's needed and wanted by the community?
Check.
A passion and heart for seeing the ministry happen?
Check.
A working model of what the ministry will look like?
Check.
Then all that was left was to call a contractor, spend a little money, and slice through the grand opening ribbon with one of those giant pairs of scissors, right?
Wrong.

*D*enny Harris is the former executive pastor of McLean Bible Church and the founding chairman of the board of Jill's House. He was on the front lines when the time came to move from dreaming about building an overnight respite care facility to actually getting the thing built—and it was an uphill climb.

As your church moves forward with a respite care ministry, you're not looking to raise a building. Truth be told, your friends at Jill's House wouldn't necessarily recommend you go that route, even though they did.

"We don't envision a whole string of Jill's House facilities springing up around the country," said former Jill's House Director of Communications Andy Krispin. "It could happen, but that's not something many churches have the capacity to do."

Plus, Andy points out, wouldn't it be better if, rather than a few churches investing in building facilities, hundreds or thousands of churches worked with the buildings they already have? It would multiply the ministry exponentially and make respite care available in far more locations.

So why explore how the Jill's House facility got built?

It's because the team at Jill's House learned a remarkable amount as they went through the process. And while you may not need to do as much to get your ministry launched, you'll have to cover a lot of the same ground.

You, too, will have to think through facility considerations, crafting communication, figuring out funding, and getting buy-in from stakeholders.

And you have to do it all while not letting your passion for sharing God's love get sidetracked while attending to the mountain of details. The Jill's House team kept their vision of sharing God's love through respite care foremost in mind as they navigated building their ministry—and they'd urge you to do the same.

Because the point isn't just respite care, as valuable as that is in the lives of families. It's pointing those families toward the source of lasting rest: Jesus Christ.

"There were significant obstacles standing in the way of creating Jill's House," said Denny, "One of them was funding and another was the approval process for building the place. Both happened in what some might say was the worst possible time and context."

McLean Bible Church had recently purchased a piece of property and was in the process of building a new sanctuary. "We were working on a church-wide multimillion-dollar capital campaign to fund that project," said Denny. "Then along we came, raising money for Jill's House. It's not a stretch to say the congregation was experiencing a little capital campaign fatigue."

And then there was the location of Jill's House.

The church had purchased the headquarters of the National Wildlife Foundation, an organization whose staff had steadily shrunk through the years.

"The Foundation had a 230,000 square foot facility and their team was rattling around in it," Denny remembers. "They needed a newer, smaller building, so they put their headquarters on the market. We bought it, understanding we'd have to add a sanctuary to the existing facility."

The building sat on roughly 51 acres, nestled into an upscale residential area. Apart from the building, the rest of the property was a wooded, oasis crisscrossed by hiking trails, a sort of neighborhood private park.

"Then along comes a church that's going to push out a 157,000 square foot building, add a two-story parking structure, and create a traffic jam every Sunday. Nobody was happy to see us show up," said Denny.

It took McLean 12 months to get permission to proceed with construction and much of that time was spent in public hearings with the neighbors. Denny assured Lon that in five years the controversy would be old history—people would be fine with the church having invaded their park and neighborhood and everyone would have moved on.

His estimate was a bit off.

"It took *11* years," remembers Denny. "And as executive pastor, it was my role to manage our relationship with the neighbors. That was the most thankless job I've ever had."

Denny was still recovering from the managing the building conflicts when the time came to add a new piece of construction to the property: Jill's House.

"We knew we'd have to go back into that same approval process and I was *not* looking forward to it," he said.

This time approval took even longer: 14 months. Denny's convinced it might have gone quicker had the team been able to more crisply communicate their vision for what Jill's House would become.

The value of communicating—often

"We knew what we were dreaming of doing, but we couldn't articulate it clearly," he said. "It's understandable that if we couldn't describe exactly what we meant by 'respite care facility' then our neighbors would fill in the blank, defaulting to stereotypes of what it might mean."

Some neighbors imagined the facility would be a mental institution and wanted to know how high the fences would be so no residents could escape and wander into the neighborhood. Other neighbors were concerned about how Jill's House would keep drugs used to treat the residents secure and feared rising crime rates as felons attempted to break into the facility to steal narcotics.

Denny just shook his head. "When you know who we serve at Jill's House, you know the *last* thing you need is a fence. But our neighbors didn't know that...and we could have done a far better job telling them."

In the end, Jill's House got approval for construction. "We won—but we didn't win any friends," said Denny.

When Jill's House finally opened its doors, it held an open house for parents, families, and members of the special needs community.

"Then someone—I wish it would have been me—suggested we should invite the neighborhood," said Denny. "My first reaction was that I didn't want to spend one more minute with them, but it was a good idea and we held the open house. As one of our staff walked a group through the facility I trailed along behind. That's when I heard someone just ahead of me turn to another neighborhood leader and marvel, 'Do you realize the church *paid* for all of this? They *did* that?'"

Denny said the comment wasn't completely true—there were donors from outside McLean Bible Church—but illustrates the turn around that happened when people understood what the church was doing.

"When I left my job at the church, one of the guys who gave me the warmest goodbye was someone I would have called a nemesis while we were creating Jill's House," said Denny.

Had Jill's House provided better information up front to the neighborhood, it may have significantly reduced friction. Communicating early, clearly, and consistently would have been worth its weight in gold—and saved Denny some battle scars.

The same is true for you as you launch your respite ministry.

You may not be bringing any earth movers and concrete trucks into the neighborhood, but you *are* inviting new people into your church building—and that can be unsettling to current church members. It's especially true if church members have little or no understanding of who you'll be serving, why you're serving them, and what it will do for your congregation.

We'll help you with that challenge. Starting in Chapter 12, you'll find sample messages you can use in church bulletins and on your church's website to communicate the benefits of a respite care ministry. Benefits to participants—and benefits to your church.

You'll have to add your own details, but you've got the essentials.

And you've got this advice from Denny: "Communicate. Communicate *lavishly*."

Take it from a guy who found out the hard way.

Figure out funding

Here's the beauty of funding a respite program you host for a few hours on a Saturday afternoon: It doesn't have to cost much in terms of infrastructure and programming.

But Jill's House has learned that simply providing a babysitting service isn't enough. The parents of children you'll host won't be able to rest until they're confident that their children aren't just safe, but also engaged and enjoying their experience with you.

And if you want the respite experience to be as much fun for children as it is their parents, you'll want to have opportunities for play and creativity—ways to make the experience a highlight for kids. That may cost a few dollars, so be aware you'll need to create a budget.

You'll also want to make sure your facility is appropriate for this ministry.

Assuming your church building is in the United States and was built after 1990, the architect may have designed the structure to be in compliance with the Americans with Disabilities Act (ADA). If so, you have a great start.

If you're not sure you're in compliance with ADA standards—and you may not be no matter how recently your building was built—see the checklist in the Appendix. You'll have a good idea where you stand after walking through your facility with that list in hand.

As far as buildings go, Jill's House started from scratch. It was a huge opportunity—building from the ground up meant being able to design a facility tailored for overnight respite care.

But that opportunity also presented a huge challenge.

Tucking a few children into a church classroom with volunteers had cost McLean Bible Church next to nothing. But building a 45-bed facility that could provide excellent overnight respite care?

That would cost a fortune—a fortune not factored into the McLean Bible Church's budget. If Jill's House was to be built, it would require funding outside the church's resources.

Yes, the church was generous and supportive, but that generosity fell far, far short of what was needed to build and maintain Jill's House. Which meant the planning team, who was uncomfortable engaging a professional fundraiser to lead the charge, shouldered a monumental task.

How big a task?

Well...they weren't exactly sure.

"We didn't know at the front end of our planning what the final cost would be," Denny said, "But the team knew it would be millions of dollars. Many millions of dollars."

Denny and the team learned plenty about fundraising as they moved the construction of Jill's House along from one step to the next. Even if you're not planning to build a facility, the lessons they learned can help you, too.

And here's one of those lessons: It takes money to fuel ministry.

"Most parents can't pay what it really costs to place a child in overnight respite at Jill's House, said Brenda Solomon. "That's why Jill's House is a non-profit with its own board, raising its own funds through donations, grants, and checks from foundations. We don't want to let a family's finances get in the way of experiencing our ministry."

Even if you're only ramping up a room with a few touch-screen tablets and some basic furniture, you'll be writing a few checks. And adaptive furniture, the sort that plays well with children of all ages and accommodates wheelchairs, isn't cheap.

Finding funding was a major emphasis for Jill's House, and the team found a range of ways to collect the dollars needed...or save on expenses. Both approaches beefed up the bottom line.

You'll find a quick primer about how to tap those sources in Chapter 15, courtesy of Denny and Jill's House.

Find a mentor

The Jill's House team traveled to Israel to shadow an organization that was doing what the team wanted to do. The advice offered and gratefully received greatly accelerated making key decisions about Jill's House.

Your mentor is hopefully not so far afield, but that mentor is out there somewhere...and you need to find it.

There's simply no one-size-fits-all, step-by-step manual for launching a respite care ministry. It doesn't exist. Your church is unlike any other and your community is one-of-a-kind, too.

There are common issues that arise when launching a respite ministry. Jill's House encountered them, and we're addressing them in this book and sharing the lessons we learned.

One of those lessons was that it pays to find a mentor—an organization that can help you figure out what you don't know but need to know. That will answer questions and talk you off ledges and through challenges.

It may be an area church that's doing respite care. It may be another sort of organization addressing the same needs you're addressing. Whoever it is, as you start making decisions, invite that mentor to speak into your vision for respite care. If your mentor is local, ask that mentor what's already available in your community and what's most needed. Ask about the best places to get training and information.

Pay attention to their answers and also their heart. If you're a match, it's a satisfying relationship for all concerned.

So find a mentor. If you struggle to locate one, check in with Jill's House to see what suggestions your friends there might have for you. Also, use the expertise of members of your congregation and people in your community who might be able to answer questions regarding medical, legal, fundraising, and even potential regulatory issues.

Here's something Jill's House will quickly tell you if you call: While parents raising children with disabilities may have advice to share, don't rely on them to do much to get the ministry up and running.

"Many Jill's House families have said that when they've approached their pastors with a request for a special needs classroom or respite care program those pastors have said, 'Sure, go ahead,'" said Andy. "This puts the burden back on parents who are already stressed out and at their limit. You need buy-in from other members of the community."

At minimum, as you look for insight about how to move forward, visit ministries like the one you're hoping to create on "snoop trips." Poke around, interview team members, ask about why decisions were made as they were made. Spend a lot of time asking, "Why?"

It's worth going the distance for a dose of inspiration and information. Jill's House has received teams from as far away as the Ukraine and China.

Get buy-in from stakeholders

A key question to answer as you look to launch a respite care ministry: Who needs to approve what you'd like to do?

And a second question that comes trotting along right behind it: Who might fire a torpedo as you get the ministry afloat?

If your church is like most, you'll need approval from a board, session, eldership, or the local archbishop. Someone will have to sign off on your using the building and representing the respite program as a ministry of your church.

At minimum, you'll need a nod of approval from your pastor. By the way, if you *are* a pastor, reading this book as you consider launching a respite care ministry in your church, thank you!

Lon's personal experience meant he not only approved of creating a respite care program, he championed it. The reception you receive may be less enthusiastic, or you may be met with a shrug. In either case, Lon has a suggestion about how to get pastors on board.

Asked what it would have taken to recruit his support had he not had Jill in his home, Lon paused for a long moment.

"I'm not sure I'd have supported respite care," he admits. "I'd have listened to you and would have at least agreed it's a good idea. But there are a lot of good ideas out there. I'd have told you I don't see why this ministry is more worthy of support than five other ministries that have been proposed."

That Lon so intimately understood the need made a great deal of difference in his support. That the McLean Bible Church congregation had seen Brenda and Lon live out the need for respite care primed them to be equally supportive.

"People saw the pain we were going through," said Lon. "They saw me come in on Sunday morning after having been up all night tending to Jill as she seized. The church was living this with us."

Were Jill not part of the equation, what would have moved Lon isn't a compelling argument. What would have mattered was actually visiting a respite ministry and seeing what was happening with the children. He would have needed to talk with parents to hear what impact the ministry was having in their lives and marriages.

"You've got to get a pastor out of the office and to a program like Jill's House," said Lon, as he leaned into the conversation. "Once they experience the joy of caring for and being around the kids, you've got a far better chance of success than if you just ask the pastor to pray about it."

Lon tells about a pastor friend in Maryland whose church was donated a house. "I told him he could turn it into a residential respite care facility," said Lon. "He told me the high school group wanted the house and so did the junior high group. Ministries in his church were standing in line to get the place."

Lon invited—begged, actually—for his friend to come tour Jill's House. "I told him I just wanted him to look—no commitment. Just tour the place and hear what we were doing."

The pastor came, spent an hour touring, and then he and Lon took their wives to dinner. "He told us that no other group was getting the house," Lon said. "It was going to be a residential overnight respite care facility."

Nothing Lon said would have had near the power of the pastor actually experiencing respite care in action. That's what convinced him—seeing was believing.

"If you're not getting support in your church, my advice is to do whatever you need to do to take a trip to see respite care in action," Lon said. "Bring the pastor, bring the whole leadership team. Let them see what respite is and then talk."

As far as anticipating who'll have a problem with your respite care program, do this: Think about who might be afraid and what's behind their fears.

We'll put these fears to rest later, but for now just know they may be circling around, so be prepared to encounter them.

• **What about liability?** Should something happen while a child with special needs is in your building, might that result in a lawsuit?

• **Where's the health professional?** Who's adequately trained to respond to significant medical conditions?

- **What if we can't find and train enough volunteers?** When it's hard to get enough people to cover programs already in place, why would we launch something new?

- **Why create a ministry to serve people who aren't in the church?** If you build it, will they really come?

Don't worry: There are ways to respond to each of these fears—and you'll find them in Chapter 16.

If someone raises a concern, deal with it directly. Behind most fears is a legitimate concern—it's far better to get those out and on the table so you can deal with them.

And remember, by the time you come to a board to ask for approval for your respite care program, you've been thinking about it awhile. You may be hitting others cold; it will take some time for them to catch up with you.

It's absolutely worth winning stakeholders over, because you'll need each and every one of them. And, ultimately, each of them will be blessed by their coming alongside your ministry.

CHAPTER 6

A QUICK TOUR OF JILL'S HOUSE

So, when the vision for Jill's House was finally translated into walls and windows, what was it like?

First, know that with one phone call you can arrange a tour, courtesy of your friends at Jill's House. Tell them you're considering doing respite care, and they'll welcome you and walk you around for a quick peek at what they've built and what God has done.

Because you may not be up for a drive to D.C., here's a virtual tour led by one of the team members you'll want to meet if you visit: Tranitra Joyner.

You won't be visiting every corner of the facility but you'll stop by the places that make Jill's House so effective with children and their parents:

- **Activity Rooms**—where kids get to explore and express their creativity
- **Play Spaces**—where kids get to rip and roar and just be kids
- **The Chapel**—where kids hear about and meet Jesus

Along the way, we'll stick our heads into rooms to take a quick glance, always with an eye towards how you can create your own custom versions of these spaces.

But before we launch into our tour, let's start where most families first encounter Jill's House: in the Lobby.

It all starts in the Lobby...

As the Jill's House weekend supervisor, Tranitra knows every inch of the 42,000-square-foot building.

Knows it—and loves it.

That's because to her it's more than a building. It's the families and children she and the rest of the Jill's House staff have been serving since 2010.

To be fair, there's a lot to love about the building itself because walking into Jill's House is like slipping into a warm, welcoming hug.

The building is carefully designed to appeal to both children with special needs and their families, to signal that this is a place that's both safe and fun. At Jill's House, children with disabilities and delays are not only welcome—they're celebrated.

"We built this space to look like a lodge," Tranitra said, pointing out the natural woodwork and freestanding stone fireplace cheering the lobby with a perpetually dancing gas fire. Light floods the space through generous windows and comfortable seating scattered around the room invites guests to sit and relax.

Near the door hangs a large photo of Jill Solomon herself, surrounded by framed shots of clients and staff. It's an unspoken reminder that, more than anything else, Jill's House is about the people who come to be served.

Jill's House is their house, too.

As first impressions go, Jill's House couldn't be more inviting and that is crucial.

Matt McNeil remembers his first impression of Jill's House.

"I remember as we were walking in, we saw all the bricks families had inscribed in memory of someone, thanking someone, or a meaningful Bible verse. The verse that leapt off the pavement at me said, 'Come to me all you who are weary and I will give you rest.' I just can't think of a better verse to have etched into the stone of Jill's House. Everyone who comes through the doors is promised rest," Matt said. "The parents can rest assured that their kids are well cared for. Whether it's physical rest or relational healing time, they'll experience rest and restoration. And the kids will have a fantastic time of rest, play, and activity in a special place that's there for them, that's all theirs."

When a family comes on a Friday night for weekend respite care it won't be the first time the parents have been in the facility. As part of the intake process parents have already toured the building.

"But for the kiddos, this may be their first time here," said Tranitra.

And what they'll see is this: smiling faces, everywhere and anywhere they look. In addition to the front desk volunteer, a greeter is on hand to connect with children and their parents. Child care staff greet the kids they'll be serving throughout the weekend, and they're careful to engage parents, too.

What happens in the first few moments of walking into Jill's House is strategic.

"We want children to know they're in a place where they're safe and will have a good time," said Tranitra. "And the parents have to trust that we've got this—that they can trust us to care for their kids. They've got to feel comfortable with us."

Those first minutes—whether a family is at the front end of overnight respite care at Jill's House or dropping a child off for a few hours at a Saturday afternoon program—are critical. It's when a respite ministry communicates that it's organized, capable, and caring.

On a Friday evening at Jill's House, the child care staff quickly whisk kids away to visit their bedrooms, be introduced to their peers, and then engage in activities.

"Getting kids busy having fun helps alleviate any separation anxiety," said Tranitra, who notes that almost always children head off with their child care staff member without a backward glance at their parents.

"Sometimes parents will have tears in their eyes and say, 'Can I see my child again before I leave?' We'll tell them their child is fine and that their respite time has begun. Their kids are busy groovin', movin', and everything is good."

Parents briefly meet with a nurse to complete the check-in process, providing medical updates and information about medication.

"For some parents, this is the first time they've ever left their child with someone other than a relative, or for longer than a few hours," said Tranitra. "It can be hard for them to leave their child with anyone. We give parents a phone number they can call anytime they'd like to check up on their children. I tell them they can call every hour if that's what they need to do. We'll always answer and we're always fine with them calling."

Some parents come close to taking her up on her offer, at least the first time their children stay for a weekend. Others—even on the first weekend—seldom or never make a call.

"It all depends on the parent," said Tranitra. "It's whatever makes them comfortable." Jill's House offers occasional Friday night dinners for parents dropping off their children—it's another way to help ease the transition for parents and also provides an opportunity for the parents to form community.

Constant access is important in successful respite care ministries, whether it's at Jill's House for a weekend or your church building for a few hours on Saturday morning. Parents of special needs children discover early on that staying in touch is more than just a good idea—it's essential.

So, if you're hosting a respite care program, have an easy way for parents to check in. It's not that they're hovering, helicopter parents; it's that the level of care they've had to provide has taught them it's wise to know what's happening with their children and to be available if there's a care-related question.

Be mindful that, for some parents, experiencing respite is as freeing as well as a bit disorienting.

Dana Hecht, vice president of family support at Jill's House, describes what she heard from one set of parents whose child's autism meant that home routines had to be strictly followed to avoid upsetting their son.

"What they enjoyed most about their respite weekend were things that might, at first, seem insignificant," said Dana. "But they certainly weren't insignificant to those parents."

Rather than having to back their car into the driveway, as their son insisted, they could pull straight in. And because having anything hanging on the banister upset their son, for years they'd never been able to drape a coat or scarf there.

"They spent the weekend feeling like rebels, because they could pull straight into their driveway and toss their coats on a banister," said Dana.

Activity Rooms
Let kids be kids—give them the fun of exploring and expressing their creativity!

Creativity Creek is the Jill's House art room, and a quick glance around confirms that if any craft supply has been invented, it's found its way here.

Framed art from previous visitors brightens the walls, as well as murals and paintings. Low tables, covered with plastic, become easily-cleaned canvases for a wide range of art projects.

And well-organized cabinets are filled with bins of...well, everything.

"This is where children come to cut, glue, color, craft, and create," said Tranitra. "There's a ton of paper around, plus pipe cleaners, cotton balls, crayons, markers, paint—pretty much everything you need to do art."

Staff often place samples of simple art projects on the tables, inviting children to make their own versions of what they see. But there's zero pressure—kids are equally welcome to do something else using any of the supplies they find...including glitter.

"Glitter," sighed Tranitra. "It gets everywhere. It's here in the art room and then gets tracked through the building and even follows you home. But the kiddos love it, so we've got glitter."

Key to the success of Creativity Creek is the staff's ability to select appropriate art projects and then not insist that children stick to the script. "We give kids lots of choices," Tranitra said.

Though some art projects are both intentional and strongly encouraged.

"Handprints and footprints or anything written to mom and dad for Mother's Day, Father's Day, or a holiday are treasures for parents," she said. "Some parents have never had an art project done by their child to hang on the refrigerator door. We make sure they have something to take home with them when they pick up their child at the end of the weekend."

Some parents hold the artwork to their chests and have tears in their eyes. "It means a lot to them," Tranitra said.

Even kids who aren't up for crafts have something fun to do in Creativity Creek.

"Kids love playing with the sparkly moon sand," said Tranitra, pointing to bins of treated sand that let kids easily craft sand castles and sculpt shapes. Tucked in the bins are toy dinosaurs, balls, and random objects so children can create dioramas and landscapes.

"These kiddos have amazing creativity," Tranitra said. "We get to help them express it."

Technology Trails is equipped with six touch-screen tablets with headphones along with several small computers. The technology sits on low wooden desks easily accessible with wheelchairs or by pulling up one of the sturdy wooden chairs.

When Jill's House was planning this room, a team did deep-dive research to find software that would be especially friendly to children with disabilities. At some considerable expense it was installed—and then promptly ignored.

What kids enjoyed was drawing on screen and then printing out the art they created using an off-the-shelf software program. And what they *really* wanted to do was watch YouTube videos.

"Kiddos know what they want to see," said Tranitra. "Some want to watch cooking shows. Others want to watch trains. We'll have six or eight children in this room and each child will be seated at a desk focused on a screen—watching a favorite show or playing a computer game."

Staff bring activities that can be done while sitting in a chair to entertain those rare kids who don't enjoy computers.

So, if your plans for a respite care room include making tablets or touch-screen computers available, don't worry about providing a suite of educational software. It's fine if you have it, but be sure you also have a strong wi-fi connection that can accommodate streaming video.

And don't worry if technology is beyond your church's budget. Especially if you're providing short-term respite care, parents generally appreciate your encouraging their children to participate in more socially-engaging activities.

Even with the best shock-proof cases money can buy, laptops and tablets are fragile, expensive, and ultimately don't deliver as much value as keeping kids engaged with your staff, volunteers, and one another.

Cricket Symphony greets kids with a range of music-related options. There's a large selection of music videos available so kids can dance or sing along, or children can take a musical instrument from one of the cabinets and play along.

"Some kids grab ukuleles and other instruments and have an impromptu jam session," said Tranitra. And because there are kids who love playing the piano, a sturdy upright sits against one wall.

"This is a relaxing room, but an active one," said Tranitra. "It all depends what sort of music the kids want to hear or make."

Staff are always sensitive to signs of stress and constantly monitor children to make sure they're not over stimulated or reacting negatively to the sheer volume of a half-dozen children doing drum and guitar solos.

Navigating that line between an activity or space being active but not stressful is something any respite program has to do.

One discovery at Jill's House is that you can avoid many problems by carefully creating buddy groups that include children who share similar interests and abilities. Because children often come back repeatedly to enjoy what you offer, you'll quickly discover individual kids' preferences.

It's also something you can ask parents about during initial conversations.

Tranitra admits it can get loud in Cricket Symphony, but if God loves a joyful noise, this is someplace he must love visiting.

The Library

"When children come in here, they have choices," Tranitra said.

In one part of the room kids find comfortable chairs where they can sit and relax, read or at least glance through one of the books they'll find in low, wheelchair-accessible bookshelves, or complete a puzzle.

It's also a great spot for childcare staff to gather kids to listen to a book being read aloud—by either the staff member or a child.

Further into the room, near a wall of windows looking out at a relaxing green landscape, sit a mountain of foam wedges and beanbags. It's where kids snuggle up with a book or sit when they want to hear a story being read aloud, but not be directly involved with the storytelling or listening.

"We also have CD players kids can use to listen to audiobooks," Tranitra said.

Jill's House has collected hundreds of books, and it's not unusual for a child to remember a favorite book from one visit to the next.

Tranitra laughed as she told an anecdote about one child who wanted to see a specific book the child had seen on an earlier visit to Jill's House. The volunteer worked with the child to sort through literally hundreds of books looking for that one particular volume.

"That search took a while, but it gave that child and volunteer a chance to relate and share an experience," she said.

Kids choose what they'd like to do while in the library, but every choice has this in common: it's calming. Every activity is engaging and often builds community in a quiet way.

Like every other room in Jill's House, the library is strategic and inclusive. Children who may be unwelcome in other libraries, because they make too much noise, are welcomed here just as they are. And they're not only welcomed, they're *celebrated.*

At Jill's House children with special needs aren't expected to adapt to the environment—the environment has adapted to them.

Play Spaces
Let kids be kids—give them room to rip, roar, roll, and burn off energy!

The **Big Sky Gym** was built with kids in mind—from the large, colorful moon bounce to a dozen other ways to burn off energy that can be enjoyed alone or played with others.

"We have an adaptive bowling game," said Tranitra, "And we now have a two-player basketball game where kids can practice shooting free throws."

A regular backboard and hoop—one considerably lower than the regulation 10 feet—gives ambulatory children a chance to practice their dribbling and three-point skills.

Several scooters lean into one corner and some children are quick to hop on and zip around the gym.

The gym's laminate floors make movement easy, and blue pads on the lower portions of the walls soften any scooter miscalculations.

Having lots of play options available is important because, as Tranitra mentioned, "Some children are able to play together. Others are more comfortable with parallel play—they're with others who are playing, but not interacting directly."

In **Adventure Heights** the entire floor is a blue gym mat—a safe, soft surface ready for occasional tumbles. Adventure Heights is built for action, from a beanbag swing to a rock-climbing wall, to a stop sign positioned so children can play a rousing game of Red Light, Green Light.

Round pieces of foam are scattered around the floor, each looking like a colorful stepping stone. Tranitra hopped on one and the sound of a chime rang from beneath her shoes.

"These all make a different sound when you step on them," she said, as she pointed out that kids can arrange them in any order to create a signature sound. "It's like playing musical hopscotch," she laughed.

A piano keyboard on the floor also makes sounds when kids step on the keys, prompting some interesting dance moves accompanying the melodies.

Tranitra's motto for Adventure Heights—for all of Jill's House—is "safety first and lots of fun," and nowhere is it more evident than here.

Just outside the room, a brass plaque reads, "Adventure Heights: This room was donated by General Dynamics in celebration of children with special needs."

This means a company that believes in giving back to the community believed Jill's House was doing significant work worthy of support.

A question: What company—or civic organization—in your area would be honored to help you fund or equip your respite care ministry? Tuck that thought into the back of your mind, and when you're reading the portion of this book about funding, see who comes to mind.

But this suggestion comes with a caution: Corporate fundraising isn't always reliable, and it may not provide all the money you need to fund an ongoing project.

The Pool shimmers in an open, sunlit room and may well be the most popular room at Jill's House.

The pool is large enough to be lap-worthy for children who can swim and was designed especially for children with disabilities.

Many public pools are both loud and crowded, two conditions that can be over stimulating for some children served by Jill's House. Plus, there's a deep end lurking not far away. Add to the mix that, at public pools, there's just one overworked lifeguard trying to keep track of dozens of frantic kids, and you've got a recipe for disaster, especially for some children with physical disabilities.

It's not hard to see why many worried parents don't take their kids swimming.

But at Jill's House it's a completely different experience.

"Our pool doesn't *have* a deep end," said Tranitra. "It's a gradual slope from two feet to three-and-a-half feet. And getting in and out of the pool isn't a big deal. Ambulatory kids can walk down three steps and everyone can get in and out using the ramp."

Tranitra enjoys describing how children unaccustomed to a pool make their way into the water.

"Our kiddos love splishing and splashing, but first you've got to get them in the pool. Some children are ready to jump right in, but others aren't so sure at first," she said. Keep in mind the water temperature is between 89 and 91 degrees, so it's warm, comfortable, and easy to acclimate. None of that jumping into freezing water stuff. And we never have more than four kids in the pool at one time, so it's not noisy and chaotic. Still, if you're not used to being in water, it's an adjustment."

Some children literally take one step down the ramp, dip their toes in the water, and stand stock still. But it's not long before they take another step and are in water up to their ankles. Then another step takes them in deeper, and eventually they'll be standing in the pool itself, the ramp behind them.

"That's when our lifeguard, Mike, may push one of the inflatable pool toys toward the child, inviting the child to play," Tranitra said. "It doesn't take long before they're having a great time."

Unlike most public pools, the Jill's House pool is accessible even to children in wheelchairs. Non-ambulatory children are transferred to a special pool wheelchair and enter and exit the water via the ramp. For perhaps the first time in their lives, they're included in a pool party—and they relish every minute.

There are no harsh chemicals used to keep the pool clean and filtered because of how they affect some children's skin. Gentler chemicals, the kind used in spas, do the trick without causing children with skin sensitivities any problems.

Children in the weekend respite program who want to go swimming can do so for 30 minutes on both Saturday and Sunday, and Tranitra can't recall many times a child has passed on the opportunity.

"You can see the excitement on the kids' faces when they come into the pool room," Tranitra said with a smile. "It's pretty neat."

The **Outside Play Area** is another kid-favorite spot at Jill's House.

Like the pool, it's designed with Jill's House kids in mind. And designing a play area that can accommodate both a young child in a wheelchair and a teenager with cognitive disabilities—that was a challenge.

But to watch kids light up as they come through the doors and spread out to play confirms that Jill's House got it right. There are loads of options and, depending on a child's interests and abilities, there's something for everyone.

"We have kids who love to swing," said Tranitra, "But at a public playground they may not fit in or be transferred to the swings."

Not a problem at Jill's House. There's a wheelchair accessible swing and chair swings sized for larger children. Any child who wants the experience of having the wind in his hair can have it and have it safely.

"Some kids love taking a bike ride on our side-by-side bikes, Tranitra said. "They sit next to a volunteer and, as they pedal past on one of our trails, you see huge grins on both faces."

Those tandem riders share the trail with children on oversized big wheels and kids who are just taking a stroll.

Other children gravitate to a self-powered adaptive spinning wheel nicknamed the "Jill's House Merry-Go-Round." Or they use the slides, balance beam, jungle gym, or monkey bars.

Tranitra pointed out the rock-climbing tunnel. It's exactly what it sounds like: a tunnel kids can climb through while others climb up, on, and over it.

A stretch of lawn makes for summer fun when a few soccer balls are waiting for children or a sprinkler is turned on to invite water play.

Like nearly every space at Jill's House, there's choice built into the play area. Kids engage with those activities they enjoy rather than have a regimen dictated to them. And because there are so many options, children are almost never bored.

Even if a respite care program doesn't have all these adaptive options available, that key insight of providing options can guide what *is* provided. Almost any outdoor space can become an impromptu soccer field or basketball court or—even better—both. Inflatable balls for catching and throwing work with children in or out of wheelchairs. Bubble blowing and chalk drawing on sidewalks may seem simple, but they're fun—and kids of all ages can give them a try.

And if you can get your hands on a set of plastic containers, you're well on your way to having one of the most popular stops on the Jill's House playground: the drum set.

They're heavy-duty plastic containers that can take a beating which is handy—because that's what they take often—and with gusto.

A recent addition to the drums is a sound box that lets kids record their singing and drum playing and then play them back. It's percussive karaoke and kids line up to give it a try.

The Chapel
Let kids be kids—and have the joy of meeting Jesus!

The Chapel sits just to the left as guests step into the lobby. It's a calm room, aglow with colored light filtering in through three large stained-glass windows.

"Chapel services are led by Mr. Brad," said Tranitra. "He started at Jill's House as a volunteer and now works here. But he comes in an hour and a half before his shift on chapel days to lead the three half-hour services."

Chapel is available every Saturday and Sunday for children in residence, though attending services isn't mandatory.

"Because we serve people of different faiths or no faith, we don't require kids to come to Chapel," said Tranitra. "Parents, or the kids themselves, decide if they're comfortable attending chapel."

The overwhelming majority of parents are fine with this part of Jill's House programming, though a few have preferred to have their children spend time in the library during chapel times.

When not in use for chapel services, the room is opened as a spot kids can come to relax. A keyboard in one corner is seldom used during chapel services, but between services it gets a workout.

"We have one child who comes to Jill's House who can play anything and everything by ear," said Tranitra. "When he visits, he loves coming in here to play the keyboard."

And Jill's House staff love hearing the impromptu concerts.

Brad Phillips was drawn to helping lead chapel because 30 years earlier, while he was working as a youth pastor, he was asked to lead a worship service for children with disabilities.

"I had no idea what I was doing," Brad remembers, "And when I asked about a manual to help me get started, I was told there wasn't one. But that time helped prepare me for what was coming later."

What came was a son with severe autism—and a heart for children with special needs.

Chapel services are brief, and no more than a dozen kids are in each service. Having three services back-to-back allows for keeping the gatherings intimate and focused.

Through the years, Brad has fine-tuned how he designs the services.

"I build in four elements," he said. "We pray, sing songs, hear God's Word, and receive a blessing."

And through it all, Brad maintains a calm that radiates through the room. "We have fun because kids are kids," he said. "But these children have incredibly stressful lives. Everything is stacked against them. Many can't talk, people constantly move them from place to place, or they can't get what they want."

Chapel isn't a place for children to just *hear* there's peace in Jesus, Brad maintains—they have to *feel* it, too.

"I know I'm doing my job right when kids are smiling and participating," he said. "Occasionally a child will fall asleep—and that's okay, too."

Brad has found it's best to have a handful of songs that are used often rather than constantly introducing new music and expecting participation. Children come to associate specific songs with Chapel and participate with greater enthusiasm if they're familiar with the music.

"This Little Light of Mine," "He's Got the Whole World in His Hands," and the "Jill's House Hello Song" are usually in rotation, as are a half-dozen more favorites. Brad will introduce a new song if it connects with the day's theme, but he makes sure the song is easy to understand.

Brad's talks are between four and five minutes long, which means he works hard to stay on point. "It's a creative challenge to reduce a topic to a simple truth," said Brad. "But I do it—and that truth always has something in it that reminds us that God loves us."

Something that's helped keep Brad's sermons intriguing is his use of the "Jill's House Bible," an oversized Bible lookalike he created by taping together two box lids.

Brad tucks an object inside that leads into or reinforces his Bible point and dramatically pulls it out when the time is right.

He also sometimes incorporates a simple craft project if it helps cement the learning of the point he has in mind.

"Around Valentine's Day kids made paper hearts that said, 'Jesus Loves Me.' They had those to take home when the weekend was over as a reminder they're loved," said Tranitra.

Chapel services typically end with Mr. Brad pulling out a bubble wand to blow "blessing bubbles."

"I tell children that God is always sending blessings our way, but we sometimes don't see them," said Brad. Using the kind of bottled bubble juice on the shelf of every Dollar Store, he blows bubbles toward each child.

Some kids can catch the bubbles. The others have fun watching bubbles float around the room or land in their laps.

Mr. Brad then goes around the room placing a hand on each child's shoulder and giving that child a blessing. It's a touching moment—and a powerful one.

Asked what advice he has for others who are designing worship times for children with special needs, he offers this advice:

Create an environment conducive for the experience. "A room that's too big or too crowded is a distraction," he said, recommending that the worship experiences be kept intimate.

Don't blast the music. It's common in some circles to crank the volume up to 10, but when worshipping with children with disabilities, stay mindful that a loud, chaotic environment can be upsetting.

Maintain a calm affect. Given the nature of the children you'll serve, a worship service may be punctuated with interruptions, but don't add to the problem by expecting children to always sit quietly. "I've found the best demeanor for me to maintain is one that looks a lot like Mr. Rogers," said Brad.

Accepting, generous, kind, and compassionate. That's the look and feel you're after as you lead a Chapel service.

Make Bible stories experiential. If you're talking about Jonah, have kids rock back and forth on the "boat" you've made with chairs. Daniel on the docket? Time to have kids roar their "roar-iest," as lions in the den.

Pay attention to see if you're connecting. Like all children, children with disabilities aren't likely to stick with you if you become overly complicated or wander into the weeds. "When you're working with kids, you're in the awareness business," said Brad.

Respect the children. Brad doesn't make the mistake of speaking down to kids, because again and again, he's discovered children with intellectual disabilities take in far more than it may appear at first glance.

That's something he learned when serving typically-developing children. *All* children can surprise you with their insights, and Brad is surprised frequently.

"I bless each child at the end of Chapel," Brad said. "But I never dreamed I was also teaching children to give blessings themselves."

More than once, children have put their hands on Brad's shoulders and blessed him. "I may not have been able to understand what they were saying, but they were blessing me," said Brad. "And I'm sure God understood."

You may not have anyone come to mind who can immediately slip into a "Mr. Brad" slot. That's okay—you *do* have someone who can grow into that role. It takes time to become comfortable speaking to a group of children who don't appear to be listening or participating.

But if in all aspects of your respite ministry you pray for the Lord's provision, and trust the Holy Spirit to minister to the children in a way you may not see, you can be confident your chapel experiences are having an impact.

Tips from the tour

On the walk back upstairs to the lobby, Tranitra explains that groups of children follow a schedule that has them rotating through rooms multiple times in a day, spending 20 or 25 minutes in each location.

"Each time kids cycle through our staff tries to make the visit exciting, giving kids a unique experience," she said. "Kids will come to the Creativity Creek multiple times in a day, but we'll have something different for them to do each time. Though some kids want to do the exact same thing they always do; it depends on the child."

Tranitra's aware that someone taking this tour of Jill's House might walk away convinced that creating a respite care ministry is out of reach— *way* out of reach. But she's quick to point out that someone setting up a space in a church basement can deliver much of what Jill's House delivers— just on a smaller scale and without overnight care being in the mix.

"You can set up an art table anywhere, and a makeshift musical room is any corner where you have some instruments, a screen, and a DVD player ready to move and groove," she said "Toss a couple beanbag chairs in another corner with a few touch-screen tablets, and you've got a computer area as well. You can definitely duplicate this on a smaller scale."

What are the lessons a church starting a respite care program can learn walking through Jill's house?

There are plenty.

• **First impressions matter**

From your advertising to signage, to smiles on the faces of your team members, *everything* about your respite care experience has to radiate excellence and warmth. You're asking parents to entrust to you the most precious thing in their lives: their vulnerable children.

So, think through how you'll signal that you're confident and capable. It's unfortunate but true: Trust is hard to gain and easy to lose, so starting strong with building trust is important.

Jill's House works hard to make walking through the door on Friday night nothing short of a homecoming experience. Kids are welcomed, parents are welcomed, and the entire experience is streamlined so fun starts immediately for children and respite starts as quickly as possible for parents.

Avoiding a situation where families are standing around waiting is important: Those are moments anxiety ramps up in both parents and children. But if you quickly whisk kids away to start participating in fun activities, you eliminate opportunity for anxiety—and you'll help parents focus, too.

Your careful attention to first impressions is a way you can let parents know you "get it" when it comes to their children.

"There's a huge difference between sympathy and empathy," said Dana. "Something we hear again and again at Jill's House is that parents realize we 'get it.' We sympathize—we know there are struggles that come with raising children with special needs. But we also empathize—we see the tremendous joy families we serve experience through their children.

Dana added that these parents are just like every other parent; they love their children unconditionally.

"These are parents who would never go back. If they knew going in what life would be like raising a child with special needs, they wouldn't change a thing," Dana said. They can't imagine a world without their children in it. "And they're trusting *us* with their children. It's an honor we don't take lightly."

- **Build in both structure and choice**

Some children with special needs want and need structure. Having set times for specific types of activities comforts them.

But other kids like to wander from activity to activity.

And all children love having choices.

To keep kids happy, provide structure but keep things moving. Shifting from one activity center to the next every 20 or 25 minutes provides both structure and a change of pace.

Be careful to design in choices, too. Don't force a child to do something he or she doesn't want to do.

- **Include developmentally-appropriate choices**

A child's craft project doesn't have to resemble the example held up by an adult. Music made in the music center doesn't have to stay on beat.

The goal is exploration, experience, and fun—and building relationships as volunteers and children interact and enjoy activities together.

Be sure your team memorizes the Tranitra Motto: "Stay safe and have lots of fun." Adhere to that, and they won't go wrong.

- **Make room for physical activity**

It can be difficult to create opportunities for physical activity if your respite care room is tight or you don't have access to an outdoor space. Jill's

House has an outside area that is open much of the year and a gym when snow or rain make outside play impossible.

How will you address the need for movement?

Consider making dancing a part of your music center or encouraging children to move along with the music. Touch can be touchy, so don't assume that every child will want to pair up with a volunteer and take a whirl around the dance floor.

But find some way for movement to happen in one of your rotations; it makes a world of difference for children who need to get up and go.

• **Find and train the right team**

It all starts and ends with having the right people in the right places as you do this ministry. No amount of adaptive equipment or slick programming compensates for doing what Jill's House does so well: Bring great people on board. Get people with a heart to help, a love for God, and a passion for serving others.

At Jill's House most of those people are paid staff who are assisted by volunteers. In your ministry it might be the other way around, but either way commit to excellence in choosing who participates in your program.

Which means it's possible for you to find people to serve in your respite care ministry who are every bit as good—and in the "Volunteers, Volunteers, Volunteers" chapter we'll show you how.

Don't skimp on recruitment and training—it's the very heart of your ministry.

• **Pair up people**

Tranitra makes sure volunteers and the children they'll be serving are a good match. Some of that is knowing the strengths of your volunteers, and some is knowing what the needs of the children are.

"At first it's an educated guess," said Tranitra. "But as kids come back and we get to know them better, it's easier to line them up with the right child care staff member."

Tranitra also makes a note if specific children seem to get along especially well. She'll then put them in the same rotations as they go to activities.

- **Be intentional (and patient) about faith-sharing.**

The most effective moment to share your faith is when someone asks you about it. And if you're living your faith out through service, trust us—a question will come.

When you're loving someone's child, that disarms even parents who walk through the door feeling defensive.

Tricia Schmehl wouldn't say she was defensive, but she did carry a healthy dose of skepticism with her when she first visited Jill's House.

She wasn't quite sure what would be expected of her or her daughter if Katie were to spend a weekend at Jill's House.

"I was leery—very, *very* leery," Tricia said. "I wondered what I was getting myself into."

But to Tricia's amazement, there was nothing to fear.

"In all the years we've worked with Jill's House—and with McLean Bible Church when Katie attended Break Away—there was never one time that I felt pushed. Instead, there was a gentle, quiet offer that lingered in the background," she said. "I'd be told a prayer service was planned and if I wanted to join in, I was invited. I'd get an email or call occasionally. But there was never—not once in over ten years—a time I felt pressured."

That quiet offer humming in the background appealed to Tricia, who hadn't ever considered attending McLean Bible Church.

"I found myself thinking, *Maybe I should check this place out*," she said.

CHAPTER 7

THE MEDICAL SIDE OF RESPITE CARE

*V*irginia O'Connell serves as the nursing supervisor at Jill's House, but her first contact with the organization wasn't at a job interview.

"I have five children, and when the youngest was heading off to college, my kids asked me what I planned to do with my time," she said.

Virginia told them she'd figure it out.

"I was at the pool one day and someone heard me talking about having an empty nest. She knew I loved kids and said, 'You've got to check out Jill's House.' It sounded interesting, so I came for a visit."

One visit and she was hooked. Virginia began volunteering and then started adding more and more volunteer shifts. It wasn't long before she was on board full time.

"I love it," she said. "Often, when parents first bring their children for a weekend it's the very first time they've left their children with a caregiver overnight. They've slept under the same roof or even in the same bed with their children for years."

But not every child whose family needs respite care is a good fit for Jill's House.

Some children's medical characteristics mean they can't be safely served at Jill's House. Some kids are experiencing behaviors that are unpredictable and make it unsafe for them to participate.

"Saying we aren't able to provide a service is seldom an issue," Virginia said. "Parents aren't looking to drop off a medically fragile child and then hope for the best. They love their kids and are very willing to discuss the level of care available here. It's not offensive to say, 'We want to welcome you but need to make sure we have adequate training to love and care for your child.'"

Parents of special needs children are used to having that sort of conversation. What they may *not* be used to is that at Jill's House—and hopefully your respite care ministry as well—the goal is to get to a "yes," rather than a "no."

"We want to serve every family we can possibly serve," said Virginia.

Virginia acknowledges that some churches might hesitate to launch a respite care ministry, because they fear the challenge they can't handle. And it's true that parents find it reassuring that while their children are at Jill's House for a weekend there's a nurse on duty.

But Virginia is quick to put a church's fear about running into medical emergencies into perspective.

"There's a possibility that *any* child in your care—special needs or not—can have a medical issue arise," she said. As a veteran mom of active children, she knows all too well that a slip off a slide or tumble down the stairs can happen whether or not a child has special needs.

"Keep in mind that in many school systems there are no doctors or nurses at schools attended by children with special needs," she said, citing certain districts that are in proximity to Jill's House. "In those facilities there are moms who got a few weeks' training from the health department and they do a fine job. And if something significant happens they do what any church can do: Call emergency services at 911."

While it's clear Virginia would like to help every family that could benefit from a stay at Jill's House, there are children who simply can't be included in an overnight respite program.

"Some kids need 24/7 individual nursing care and as much as their parents could use respite, we can't provide it," said Virginia.

Having a conversation about what a respite care ministry can and can't handle is important early on, cautions Virginia. "It's discouraging for parents to be deep into the intake process, only to discover their child was never going to be accepted into the program."

The intake procedure Jill's House has in place for an overnight stay is far more comprehensive than what you'll need if you're providing a few hours of respite care at your church. But there *are* key pieces of information you'll want to collect before parents bring a child to your facility. A basic intake form you can modify to your situation is in Chapter 17. Let that prompt your initial discussions with parents, as together you decide if your program can meet the needs of their children.

And since you're learning from the best in this Flagship Series, here are a few pointers Virginia would share with any church launching a respite care ministry, however modest it might be.

• **Be sure you know how to respond to behavioral issues, too.**

When Jill's House opened, Virginia remembers that the team hadn't received adequate training in this area—and it showed. "We ran into an incident, and though it turned out fine, we looked at one another and said, 'Ok—we need to know more about how to deal with *that.*'"

They now know, and it's a standard part of training.

For the sake of your team and the children you serve, gain skills in helping a child deal with emotions in a positive way. Some children are prone to aggressive behavior as a result of anxiety, fear, or feeling overwhelmed. Understanding how to respond appropriately helps everyone stay safe.

Contact your local school system, the Health Department, and the appropriate departments of a local university to ask what resources they might offer. Network through healthcare providers and ask families with special needs kids where they've received training.

Each time you encounter someone who might be able to help, ask for that help. Someone will be willing to invest in preparing you to serve the special needs community in your area as you provide respite care.

• **Ask questions—lots and lots of questions**

"There's a learning curve when it comes to discovering how to take care of kids with special needs," said Virginia, "And you can't offer their families respite unless you can care for their kids."

Virginia recommends doing some homework before opening your respite program. Visit other respite ministries to see what they're doing and find out what they've learned. Pick up the phone to call those too far away to visit. Ask what you should know. Ask what you should know that you don't know enough to ask about. Soak up all the information you can and learn from the experience—and mistakes—of others.

And, yes, as mentioned before, Jill's House is open to getting those calls and receiving those visits. "We hear from churches all the time," she said. "We're happy to help if we can."

There are other organizations prepared to offer assistance, too—find out more about them in Chapter 24.

- **Talk with parents**

"The parents we serve want communication," said Virginia. "They want to talk about their kids. They want community. They're eager to talk with someone who has some idea what their life is like."

Which means you may find that, when parents drop off their children for a Saturday morning, those parents don't want to leave immediately. They may linger because having a sympathetic ear is the beginning of the respite they so desperately need.

Virginia sometimes finds herself in those sorts of conversations and always finds herself in awe of how well parents of special needs children care and advocate for their children.

"I can't understand how they do it," she marvels. "I don't know how they manage to care for their kids and still have jobs. Or where they get the energy. It's amazing to me."

It probably shouldn't have come as a surprise to Jill's House staff, but early on, they discovered the first weekend parents leave their children isn't all that refreshing for those parents. They aren't able relax, because they're sitting by the phone waiting for a call.

Parents with a special needs child often become accustomed to getting a call asking them to come pick up their child halfway through the birthday party, or the field trip, or the neighborhood outing. Someone who thought they could care for their child discovers otherwise.

So even though Jill's House *looks* legit, these parents don't feel safe planning a date or night out of town—not until Jill's House has proven capable of taking care of their children well.

Talking with parents—both before *and* after their child's time in your respite care program—helps accelerate that trust-building.

So, don't be offended that parents don't automatically assume you're competent; they've been disappointed before.

And they'll be delighted you can deliver what you promise.

• **Respect the ratios**

It's important you become comfortable with this fact: There will always be more need for respite care in your community than your ministry can provide.

Which means the demand will always exceed your ability to meet it—and that may tempt you to stretch your caregivers thin to accommodate one more child, to offer respite to one more family.

Resist the temptation.

"The ratio of staff to children matters a great deal," said Virginia. It's one reason Jill's House is so careful to identify the needs of each child before that child is scheduled for a weekend.

There are children who can be cared for relatively easily—one caregiver can adequately care for two or three children. But other kids require a one-to-one caregiver ratio, and when those children are present, you simply can't serve as many children.

"You've got to be prepared to deliver everything with excellence," said Virginia. "And you can't do that when you're short-staffed."

At Jill's House ratios are based on a child's medical history, their behavioral characteristics, and their current medical requirements—all of which are explored during the intake process.

• **Pick your timing carefully**

"If you host a program that runs between 11:00 a.m. and 3:00 p.m., or noon to 4:00 p.m., you'll have an easier time of it than if you start early in the morning or go later into the evening," said Virginia. "Most kids take their meds in the morning or at night, so your team won't have the responsibility of medication."

Plus, if parents are looking for respite care because they have appointments to make and keep, or need to get projects done, they'll prize having respite hours come during the business day.

Because the stays at Jill's House stretch over several days, administering medications is a fine-tuned, highly-precise operation. There's simply no way to avoid storing medications and distributing them on a carefully controlled schedule.

Hosting your respite care program midday, or abbreviating the length of the care you provide, allows you to eliminate that process for most of the kids you'll serve.

"But don't underestimate how helpful having even a few hours free is for parents," said Virginia. "They're grateful for any hours they get."

- **Expect your heart to melt**
  While not an actual medical diagnosis, it's real nonetheless.

Virginia, whose nursing background includes stints in high-pressure, quick-response Intensive Care Units, will be the first to tell you she can switch into "Professional Nurse with Thick Skin Mode" when the situation calls for it.

But at Jill's House, she's constantly bumping into moments that melt her heart.

Moments like when a father comes beaming into the room to announce his 12-year-old has at last learned to say, "Bye."

Moments like when a parent breaks down in tears because finally, at last, she'll be able to have a full night of sleep so she can find the energy to keep going.

And moments like when a non-verbal child who can't see, reaches up to stroke Virginia's cheek and then breaks into a wide smile, because he recognizes his friend.

"Those are the times I know: I'm exactly where I'm supposed to be," said Virginia. "It's here. It's this special place called Jill's House."

CHAPTER 8

VOLUNTEERS, VOLUNTEERS, VOLUNTEERS

*W*ithout volunteers, Jill's House would struggle to provide the services it provides, and nobody knows that better than the paid staff.

Some of whom, like Virginia, started as volunteers.

And some of whom, like Tranitra, rely on volunteers throughout the day.

"They're amazing," she said. "Our volunteers come through the door eager to serve and we couldn't do what we do without them. If a volunteer is assigned to a group of children who don't need much, those volunteers will take it upon themselves to find other things they can do. They keep one eye on their kids as they clean toys or pick up an area.

"We get the cream of the crop when it comes to volunteers," Tranitra beamed. "They're flexible, energetic, and have a heart to serve. They're superstars."

And they're precisely the kind of volunteers you'll be looking for as you launch your respite ministry.

It's possible your respite care ministry will be entirely staffed by volunteers and that's not a bad thing—provided you find the right people and get them into the right spots. We'll help you do that, but first let's take a quick look at where volunteers serve at Jill's House and how they're brought on board.

First, the volunteer roles:

- **Group Buddies** directly serve the children who come to Jill's House.

    Their primary role is to assist a caregiver by engaging with two to four children, assisting with play time in the gym or on the playground, making crafts, and reading books. As kids rotate through different rooms, their Group Buddy is with them, helping them participate, stay safe, and have fun.

Group Buddies are buddies in more than name only; they get to know the children with whom they've been paired.

- **Kitchen Helpers** prepare meals and snacks for the kids.

Given the wide range of children's diets and restrictions, volunteers in this role do far more than slap together sandwiches and pile mac n' cheese on plates.

They carefully ensure that individual children receive exactly the foods they need in a timely fashion. They serve while maintaining both high levels of cleanliness and meticulous attention to detail.

By the way, you can do what many respite programs do: have parents pack food for their kids. That way you aren't responsible for preparing the food and you ensure that each child has a meal he or she likes!

- **Administrative Helpers** assist the Jill's House office staff with everything from mailings to data entry, filing to computer work.

Given the nature of the work, this is a role that requires on-site hours worked between Monday and Friday, 8 a.m. to 5 p.m.

This essential role is perfect for volunteers who do want to accomplish important tasks for Jill's House but don't want to have direct care responsibilities for children.

- **Weekend Receptionists** are responsible for greeting families as they drop off or pick up their children for a weekend stay.

Receptionists direct parents to the sign-in sheet and assist with other check-in/check-out responsibilities.

But there's another task that's essential, too: Receptionists beam warmth and reassurance to worried parents and uncertain children. They radiate the love of Jesus.

- **Chapel Helpers** help share the Gospel.

Chapel activities may include prayer, singing, Bible reading, and bubble blowing.

Here's a spot for volunteers who are both passionate about their faith in Christ and comfortable interacting directly with children with special needs.

- **Morning Helpers** serve during the Jill's House school-year program (more about that later) and make beds and clean the living areas after kids leave for school.

And this is an aptly named role: The shift starts bright and early at 7 a.m., so only early birds need apply.

- **Pool Helpers** are all wet—literally. These volunteers interact with children in the Jill's House pool, serving alongside a certified lifeguard.

During a shift, these volunteers may find themselves guiding special wheelchairs around the pool, playing pool basketball, or tossing beach balls back and forth with children.

- **Event Helpers** assist at various Jill's House events, from a golf tournament, to a motorcycle ride, to a gala reception.

These volunteers may find themselves setting up and tearing down tables and chairs, registering guests, greeting visitors, helping with auctions, or giving tours.

Event Helpers are servant-hearted people who make possible fundraisers that fuel the ministry of Jill's House.

- **And then there's "Other"** and that covers a *lot* of territory.

While not an official volunteer category, someone calling friends to invite them to a fundraiser or knocking on a neighbor's door to explain what Jill's House can do for that family is every bit a volunteer—one that Jill's House may never even meet.

These volunteers help because they care—or they're called. They serve in no official capacity but serve nonetheless.

As your ministry grows and you hear about people offering this sort of support, follow back up with those individuals. See if they'd be appropriate for and willing to embrace an official role.

Becoming a respite care volunteer at Jill's House

Jill's House volunteers must be at least 16 years old and live locally—it's important they can get to their posts when they're expected to be there.

And while some organizations are eager to take on one-shot volunteers, Jill's House isn't one of them. There's a significant investment made to select and train a Jill's House volunteer, so they're asked to commit to serving at least two, three-hour shifts per month for a minimum of one year.

The volunteer selection process requires completing an online application that is reviewed by the Volunteer Program Manager, and if applicants are selected, they're required to complete mandatory volunteer training.

Before volunteers can work a shift, they're also expected to provide proof of a negative tuberculosis test taken within the last month and, if they're 18 years old or older, pay $10 for a background check that will be ordered through Jill's House.

If you're thinking, "With all those hurdles to clear, how can Jill's House possibly find volunteers?" Let us stop you there.

Each of those hurdles matters, and you'll want to install a few of your own for potential volunteers to encounter. It's how you find the right people to deliver excellence to the families you'll serve. It's how you identify the people who'll be in it for the long haul.

Some requirements in place by Jill's House are there because of state regulations, and you likely won't have to meet them in your church's respite care.

But don't skip those that make sense, including mandatory background checks for all ministry team members. And that's *all* team members—including you.

Put that requirement front and center in your volunteer expectation checklist (we've suggested what you might include in a sample on page 165) and model compliance. You're interacting with a tremendously vulnerable population, and parents need the reassurance that you've done all you can to protect their children.

Background checks are readily available from a variety of providers—check with your church's children's ministry to see if your congregation already has a relationship with a reputable provider.

Becoming a respite care volunteer at your church
Don't be afraid to set expectations when it comes to volunteers.

It would be ideal if you attracted people who are passionate about serving families who are raising children with special needs and who have experience providing respite care.

But let's be real: There's no bench full of people fitting that description just waiting to be called into the game. Which means you'll need to be open to volunteers who lack experience in special needs and respite care services.

People like Denny Harris, the McLean Bible Church executive pastor who became chairman of the Jill's House Board of Directors, for instance.

"I didn't come to my role helping with Jill's House because of a deep desire to serve the disability community and provide respite," said Denny. "I got involved because I wanted to support Lon. It wasn't that I had any problem with the disability community; it's just that I didn't have any particular draw to this sort of service."

Denny's perspective changed quickly.

"You can't be around people making a difference in the lives of such special people without finding yourself drawn in at a heart level," he said. "If you don't have a heart for providing respite care, beware: Once you get into it, the Lord will change you. And you'll discover that, if you want to be where God's working, you want to be serving in respite care."

So, be open—but selective, too. Set standards and don't waver on finding people who will be able to meet them.

Which, given the importance of volunteers in launching your ministry, is a big, big deal. And one we'll help you address.

How to find the right volunteers for your respite ministry

You may have a vision for respite care that energizes you right down to the soles of your feet. You're passionate. You're determined. You'd hold your first respite session tomorrow if you could.

Unfortunately, that's not enough. You also need a team.

A team is so important that your friends at Jill's House, when asked by a church to coach them through establishing a respite ministry, start by asking, "Where's your team?"

"When it comes to helping other churches start a respite ministry, we usually ask that there be several churches working together in a community," said Lon Solomon. "One reason is that those churches become the source for the first round of volunteers."

When Jill's House started, a large number of people were already serving next door in McLean Bible Church's special needs ministry. These individuals already understood the importance of, and had a heart for, respite care and were quick to volunteer.

"The ideal situation is that a church with a special needs program extends that ministry into respite care," said Lon. "They already have people who care about this, and respite care becomes a wonderful opportunity for people—including young people—to serve."

Having a source for volunteers is essential, but they've got to be the *right* volunteers. They've got to be the "superstars" Tranitra described walking the halls of Jill's House.

Whether you're working with another congregation to launch a ministry or your church is going it alone, how do you find, recruit, and retain that level of volunteer?

Finding volunteers, recruiting volunteers, and retaining volunteers—those are three separate but overlapping challenges.

Let's tackle them one at a time.

Finding volunteers

A question: If ten volunteers called you in the next hour to commit to serving in your respite ministry, would you know what to do with them?

If your answer isn't an unqualified "yes," don't start looking for volunteers yet.

You're not ready for them until you've got answers to the questions they're likely to ask:

- What's your ministry trying to accomplish?
- What exactly do you want me to do?
- What training will you provide to make me successful?
- What's my commitment—exactly?
- Why do you think I'm a good fit in your respite care ministry?

The first four questions you probably anticipated—they're what every volunteer who's been around the block a time or two thinks to ask. We have samples of how Jill's House answers several of those questions and suggestions about how to answer the rest, starting in Chapter 20.

But that last question deserves some thought right now.

Why? Because if you don't know who you're looking for, how will you know when you've found the right person?

Rather than put out a plea for volunteers and then figure out how to use whoever shows up, do this: Start with a firm description of an ideal volunteer and then look for people who fit that description. Don't worry about their qualifications, look at their character and qualities.

You can train someone to serve in respite care. The information needed and skills required can all be mastered.

What you *can't* do is turn someone who's, by nature, task oriented into a people person. You can't train someone to be warm, empathic, or willing to go the extra mile to serve others.

You can't train someone to have a heart for sharing God's love through respite care, a quality that shines so brightly in the team at Jill's House.

So before you set out finding volunteer superstars, know who you're after. Then create a job description for the roles you need to have filled.

Sound like a lot of work? It can be, so we've given you a head start (see page 167) to save you time and effort. And if you think creating a job description for a ministry role is hard, try running a ministry when it's staffed by the wrong people in the wrong places.

That's *truly* hard.

Once you've identified the qualities of people you want on your volunteer team and have a description of what you need those people to do, it's time to...

- **Pray for God to bring you the right people**

There's a place for everyone to serve and, if your respite care ministry is intent on serving God and those who need respite, God has gifted people who can come serve alongside you.

Ask God to nudge those people your direction—and to give you eyes to recognize them when they show up.

- **Make a list**

As you and your team create job descriptions, make a note when someone you know comes to mind. Have your team do the same.

Then sit down and, as a team, generate a list of people you think have the qualities that will dovetail with respite care.

Don't worry if the people are already busy—we all are. Or don't worry if they're serving in other areas—they probably are. Or if they've expressed an interest in respite care—they probably haven't; it's a new opportunity.

Simply ask this: If you could cherry-pick the people you think would be successful in this role because of how they're wired, who would those people be?

Put their names on a list.

- **Pick up your phone and ask**

Before you make any general announcement looking for volunteers, directly approach the people on your list and ask if they'll serve in the respite care ministry.

A phone call will work, but a face-to-face conversation is best.

Say, "I couldn't help but think of you when I was looking at this role in respite care because..." and then share what the person has said or done that convinces you they'd be a fit.

Be specific. Be positive. And ask—if you don't ask, you won't receive. You'll miss out on having a strong team and the people on your list will miss out on the opportunity to experience joy serving in such a rewarding way.

If you hear, "no," don't cross anyone off your list. A "no" isn't forever. Stay in touch, invite those people to visit once you're up and running, and let them know the door is always open should they have time and interest in the future.

- **Then, if you still need volunteers, spread the word**

Network within your church and—if you're willing—beyond your church membership. Use your first volunteers to spread the word within their own networks. Volunteers recruiting other volunteers works well.

Jill's House is about more than providing respite care—it's about sharing the love of God *through* respite care. If you have a similar vision, be careful to expressly say so in whatever information you broadcast about seeking volunteers.

Potential volunteers need to know there's a spiritual component, and it's specifically Christian in orientation. That said, Christians are everywhere, so share what you're doing with the local Lions Club, the Rotary, men's and women's community groups, college ministries, and alumni organizations.

Contact other churches, too.

You may well find spiritually-compatible volunteers in any or all those spots.

Jill's House has volunteers who come from throughout the community, not just from McLean Bible Church. There are students who want to fulfill their required service hours someplace they know they're making a difference, grateful friends and family of children who've passed through Jill's House, or college students who are studying special needs disciplines and are eager to get hands-on experience.

They can all apply and all be considered for placement.

True of Jill's House...and true of your respite care ministry.

- **But please...don't settle**

  If you can't find the right volunteers or enough volunteers, don't launch your respite ministry until you've located them.

  The families you'll serve deserve your best—be sure you give it to them.

Recruiting Volunteers

The most effective way to recruit a volunteer has already been mentioned: asking someone to serve.

Sticking a blurb in a church bulletin isn't asking.

Neither is making a mention from the pulpit, posting a notice on a bulletin board, or sending a blanket email to your church roster.

It takes *asking*—and also removing obstacles that may be between your potential volunteers and their agreeing to sign on.

Here are common objections to volunteering—and what you can do to whittle them down to size.

"I don't have the time."

One solution to this issue is, when possible, to be flexible with timing of volunteer roles.

The Administrative Helpers at Jill's House need to come in sometime between 8:00 and 5:00 p.m., but it's not mission critical when they put in their three-hour shift.

A receptionist has to be on duty when families arrive—there's no wiggle room on the timing.

In your respite care ministry, be sensitive to noting when volunteer roles are and aren't time-critical. Do you really care when an email is sent out to your contact list about an upcoming retreat or special event? Probably not, and if that's the case, say so. Someone who doesn't mind passing up a few television shows for a worthy cause can cover that task in the evening at home.

"I'm afraid I don't have what it takes to be successful."

This is often code for "I'm afraid."

Which, truthfully, isn't a bad thing.

A bit of tension about taking on the volunteer role indicates its being taken seriously; it's an invitation to provide further information to outline the training that will be given and describe the safety net under the volunteer as he or she serves.

Volunteers interacting with children at Jill's House do so alongside a trained caregiver; the safety net is literally standing in the room.

Don't hear "I'm afraid" as a "no," because it's not. It's an opportunity to say, "I'd like to tell you why I think you'll be successful. Would you let me do that before you make a final decision about serving?"

"I'm concerned about how long I could do this."

Awkward truth: Many volunteers in the church have been taken advantage of. They've signed up to teach a class, only to discover that also involves writing the curriculum, baking the snacks, and vacuuming the room.

Plus, they had no idea they were signing on for a lifetime commitment.

The antidote to this objection is to have in hand a solid job description and a firm timeline. Be able to talk specifics—including when the volunteer can wrap up the commitment and walk away feeling something other than guilt.

At Jill's House, the volunteer commitment is for a minimum of one year. At the end of that year, a volunteer can leave and be warmly thanked on the way out the door. It's mission accomplished.

One good thing about having a firm timeline is that you'll know when to check back with the volunteer to see if signing on for an additional year is desired. Retaining a volunteer takes far less effort than recruiting and training one, so you'll want to make check-ins a regular occurrence.

To help with that, we've provided a sample Volunteer Evaluation Form for you in Chapter 20.

"Couldn't this be better done by paid staff?"

No doubt a squad of trained special needs teachers would find it a breeze to tackle the roles you're looking for volunteers to fill.

And some ministries have chosen to hire key positions rather than count on volunteers. If your budget allows full- or part-time staff, that's something to consider.

But many more ministries rely on volunteers—and it's enough. The heart they bring to training and service more than compensates for their lack of professional credentials.

"I'm not sure what I'm getting into."

Even with a job description in hand, some potential volunteers are queasy about committing until they see firsthand what they're expected to do.

So show them.

If you've not yet launched a respite ministry, take them to see one that's up and running. If you're already providing respite, let them visit to see your program in action. Just be sure they meet the criterion for being present while children are present.

Which leads to...

"About that background check..."

Everyone has a past and sometimes that past is...unfortunate.

Decide up front what discoveries made during a background check will and won't keep someone from volunteering in your respite program. Not every arrest is of equal magnitude. A night in jail for setting a sofa on fire back in college isn't the same as doing a decade in prison for assault.

If someone was caught using drugs ten years ago and doesn't use them now, is that a reason to not let the person buddy up with a child during crafts?

If someone was arrested three dozen times for speeding, could that person capably prepare snacks? (Yes...but don't let him do valet parking.)

The point: Walk the line between awareness and grace, but always keep in mind that your primary job is to protect and care for children and their families who come to your program. If you have any doubts, thank the potential volunteer and help them find another ministry in which to serve. Also be sure to check any state and local laws or regulations which might apply.

By the way, there are some logistics around giving and keeping background checks. You'll find more information in Chapter 19.

Exactly how you go about interviewing potential volunteers to ensure they're a good fit—and that they know precisely what they're signing up for—is up to you.

But there are essentials you'll want to include in the discussion and we've outlined them in Chapter 20.

For now, it's enough that you decide to have the conversation. That you review what, if anything, turned up on the background check. That you walk through expectations—yours and those of your prospective volunteer.

And that you reinforce the goal of your respite care ministry: to share the love of God through providing respite care.

Like Jill's House, you're about more than just delivering excellent care for kids—though that's undeniably important. You're about more than supporting parents with respite—though that's important, too.

Those are the "what" of your ministry. What matters even more is "why" you're doing what you're doing: You're sharing God's love as you prayerfully serve others. Your ultimate goal isn't just to provide respite, but to point others to God so they can enjoy a friendship with him as well.

Retaining volunteers

Volunteer retention starts the moment a volunteer first serves in your respite ministry.

The training you provide, the encouragement you offer, the affirmation you give—it's all part of creating an environment in which volunteers thrive and find fulfillment.

Volunteers often feel courted as they're being recruited, and then once they're serving, they're all but forgotten. There's no follow-up to make sure they're thriving in their role or that their questions are answered.

If you're looking to keep volunteers long term—and that's a wise strategy—then you've got to give them the same considerations you'd give a new employee in a job.

Those include...

Periodic evaluations

Volunteers want to know they're doing well—and, if they could do better, they're eager to find out how.

We're sometimes hesitant to evaluate volunteers for fear they'll be offended and leave. Actually, the opposite is true: If we fail to provide feedback, it signals to a volunteer the role they're filling can't be all that important.

They assume you won't miss them when they leave, because they're pretty sure you haven't noticed when they're there. Besides, easily offended people would have walked away about the time you told them they're required to have a background check.

So, sit down with volunteers and their job descriptions and talk about where they're succeeding and where they could step it up. You may discover that the volunteer is in the wrong role but wants to continue serving. Or you may uncover a concern the volunteer has that you can address.

Either way, you're communicating that the volunteer is valued.

Recognition for work well done

It's unlikely anyone signed up to serve in respite care because they're hungry for the spotlight or to receive applause. And nobody needs one more "You're a Star!" coffee cup. But we all appreciate being recognized and thanked—it's easy to leave a volunteer role if we feel unappreciated or undervalued.

So encourage. Affirm. Celebrate people—for what they do, yes, but more for who they are.

They're servants being used by God to bring hope and healing to families who need respite. They're making a difference as they use their skills and gifts to touch the lives of others.

Ask what volunteers need and how you can help

Any training you provided before a volunteer starts in a role was theoretical.

But once a volunteer has served a time or two, or experienced a difficult situation with a child, that volunteer now knows what he or she needs to know—and you have that volunteer's undivided attention.

At Jill's House, as in your ministry, training happens in real time as volunteers rub elbows with Child Care Specialists and watch how those staffers navigate situations. When a staff member in the kitchen points out how to avoid cross-contamination between foods, that's training. When an office worker walks a volunteer through how to file paperwork, that's training.

Nothing beats on-the-job training for relevance, but there needs to be more.

That more can only happen in one-on-one conversations with each volunteer. When it's just the two of you, you can ask about how the volunteer is *really* doing and what the volunteer is *really* feeling. You can ask what would make the experience of serving more rewarding for the volunteer.

You can get a sense of what's motivating the volunteer and gain insights into what kind of recognition would speak to each volunteer.

And you can discover what else the volunteer might like to contribute to your ministry. Perhaps the volunteer is an award-winning photographer whose pictures could add heart and snap to your website. Or the volunteer is a marketer who'd gladly take on advertising your ministry—but nobody has asked.

Some volunteers at Jill's House have been on board since the doors opened and that's not a coincidence.

They're treasured, and not just for what they do.

Melanie Davis is the chief administrative officer of Jill's House, but like every other staff member, she's also responsible for volunteer retention. She can't avoid it—and neither can you.

How you interact with volunteers tells them if you're glad they're there or wish you could do without them. You can influence whether volunteers see their service as the high point of their week or a task that has to be accomplished.

And it's far, far easier to be a cheerleader for your volunteers when you've taken the time to find, recruit, train, and retain people who are well-suited to serve in respite care.

"Whatever else your volunteers bring, make sure they bring a love for the kids and their families," said Melanie. It's the one intangible she's seen make the biggest difference in whether volunteers sink or swim—whether they dive in or hold back.

And whether they go the distance or quickly disappear.

"The families who come here experience so much rejection in life," said Melanie. "So often, people look at their children and then look away. But when they walk into Jill's House, they know immediately this is a place where their children will be celebrated and loved. At Jill's House their children will make friends. Through Jill's House, the parents make friends, too. Suddenly, families are connected. There's no other place families get what they get at Jill's House."

And at the very center of that experience, smiling and serving, are volunteers.

Who could be more important to the Jill's House ministry?

And who could be more important to yours?

Even if you choose to hire staff to fill key roles—and there's a lot to recommend that—you're likely to round out the roster with volunteers who'll greet guests, interact on the phone, and keep your paperwork organized and up to date.

And there's this: Your volunteers often become among your very best donors. They've seen the impact of your ministry and want to support it.

CHAPTER 9

THE RANGE OF RESPITE

*I*t's the dilemma faced by every church that owns a building: What do you do with it when it's not being used for worship services?

Will it really sit empty 90% of the time—or is there some way to keep the space busy doing ministry throughout the week?

That Jill's House is known for providing weekend respite care doesn't mean the facility sits idle throughout the week. The team doesn't just wander the halls waiting for the next Friday group to arrive.

"We partner with schools in the area that have populations of kids with disabilities to fill our program during the week," said Melanie. "Tuesdays, Wednesdays, and Thursdays, we pick kids up at school and bring them back to Jill's House so their parents can get respite for the night. We deliver kids back to school the next morning, and their parents pick them up at the end of the school day."

Plus, come summer, Jill's House is a blur of activity as summer day camps kick into gear.

These camps came into existence, explains Denny, because summer is when any community's primary provider of daytime care for children with special needs closes up shop.

"It's the schools that provide a safe place for children while parents work," said Denny. "But in the summer months, all that goes away."

Seeing the need, Jill's House developed a program that allows parents to drop off children at 8:30 a.m. as parents are heading to work. Pick-up is at 4:00 p.m.

While parents work, their children take part in a full day of swimming, music therapy, arts, crafts, and a special treat: playing with therapy animals who drop in for a snuggle and some tummy rubs.

When you're creating your respite ministry, do what the team at Jill's House did: Ask not just *what* families need, but *when* they most need it.

Some scheduling challenges faced by parents are predictable. Appointments for therapy and consultations can be scheduled in advance. A working parent's reserve of vacation and sick days may be quickly used up, but there's at least a degree of control about when a parent will be away from the job.

Emergencies are another matter and some parents experience those with surprising regularity. Parents with medically fragile children, or children whose characteristics make it difficult for friends and family to care for them, sometimes find it's hard to continue working full-time...if at all.

So, you can imagine the relief of finding respite that covers key dates on the calendar when schools are closed, but parents are expected to show up for work.

Jill's House has created programming timed to resource those pinch points: Spring Break Camp, and Christmas Camp.

As you develop your respite care program, consider when you're needed most. Regular Friday evenings or Saturday daytime sessions will certainly be welcomed, but so will a President's Day Camp—and you may draw a different group of families.

Just keep this in mind: The precise timing of the care you provide may matter less than the fact you're offering care at all.

"One critical aspect of providing respite care is parents knowing that a break is coming," said Andy. "Yes, parents need child care at specific times, but our studies at Jill's House show the greatest impact on stress reduction for families isn't the respite care itself. It's knowing they have a break coming."

Another goal of Jill's House is to encourage building community, giving the parents of children with special needs opportunities to break out of the isolation many of them experience.

When Brenda was first caring for Jill, she found it hard to get out of the house. It can be tough rounding up all the gear needed to take a healthy baby to and from the grocery store—just ask any mom who's hauling a diaper bag while also attempting to fold up a stroller and strap a squirming 1-year-old into a car seat—but taking a child with profound special needs on an outing?

Plus, if and when an emergency occurs, you're on your own.

Brenda recalls times when Jill's seizures required her to lay Jill down on the floor in a public space to attend to the crisis. And she remembers that, though some people were caring, others weren't.

"We had people walk over us to continue on their way," she said, shaking her head in amazement. "They didn't offer to help, or to get help, or even to call for assistance. They just kept walking."

No wonder Brenda stayed home—even from church.

"Building community for parents and families is important to us," said Dana Hecht, vice president of family support at Jill's House. "We host a parents' support group once a month on Sunday night during the school year. It costs a bit of money, because we have a local Mexican restaurant cater the evening, but it's completely worth it. We provide childcare while parents get to know each other and talk about various topics of interest."

There's also weekday Bible study and a book club for moms. "We don't need to provide childcare for those, because their kids are at school during the day," said Dana.

Just being with other parents who get what you're going through is respite, Dana explained. Developing a community of friends is like oxygen when you're struggling with isolation and you think nobody could possibly understand what you're living through.

Keeping the facility humming with activity is important to the team at Jill's House—it's how they maximize everyone's investment in the brick and mortar building. And it's how they get to do the most ministry possible.

But they'll be the first to tell you their building has limitations.

First, there are 45 beds and only 45 beds.

Were all the area families that need respite care to show up at Jill's House at one time, the line would stretch out the door and twice around the building; that's why families are limited to four weekend visits per year. The demand for respite care far outstrips the ability of Jill's House to provide it.

But that would be true even if the facility were twice or three times its current size. *Ten* times its size.

And, second, Jill's House sits in Tysons, a community tucked in between McLean and Vienna in northern Virginia. Families raising children with special needs drive hours to use services offered at Jill's House, but there's no way to take the building and what happens in it to those families in their own communities.

And make no mistake about it: Their communities—and yours—need access to respite care.

When Jill's House president, Joel Dillon, said you can throw a dart at a map of the United States and anywhere it lands is a community needing the services of Jill's House, he's not exaggerating.

So maybe, the team at Jill's House thought, they could do more.

And not necessarily just in northern Virginia.

Dana is always on the lookout for ways to come alongside families to provide the help they need.

Which means Dana and the other ministry-minded leaders at Jill's House are constantly considering possibilities, constantly thinking outside the box.

Which means thinking outside the building.

Jill's House Camps

With weekend programs at full capacity and hundreds of families on waiting lists, Jill's House explored an innovative approach to taking respite care way beyond the Beltway.

"All across the country there are Christian camps that lie dormant most of the time," said Denny Harris. "Someone suggested scheduling weekends at those camps, taking kids from nearby communities for the weekend and giving them a great time at camp. Parents could drop kids off on Friday and then come back Sunday evening to pick them up. That would give parents a full 48 hours of respite. Plus, the expense of pulling off a weekend of camping would be minimal compared to building another facility."

Jill's House rented a camp in a neighboring county and staff drove nine children out into the country to give the idea a try. Would it work? Nobody quite knew, but if it didn't, the group was close to home and could always turn around and head back.

"We brought our activities and philosophy of caregiving with us," said Dana. "Both the kids and their families *loved* it."

Children experienced traditional camp activities—paddling in canoes, sessions at the archery range, conquering a high ropes course, and singing songs and roasting s'mores around a campfire.

"It worked so well we continued to book the facility on weekends throughout the year as a way to increase capacity," remembers Dana.

Then, basking in the glow of a success that was clearly something Jill's House could and should continue, someone asked a question that pushed the project into overdrive: If Jill's House could pull off a camp in northern Virginia, could they do it somewhere else?

And that was the beginning of Jill's House taking respite care to the national level.

Jill's House currently holds camps in four locations—Seattle, Nashville, Chicago, and at the original camp site in Virginia.

When Jill's House holds a camp in Seattle, they don't put everyone at Jill's House on a plane to go staff the camp.

"We hire staff there," said Dana. "At each location we have a Local Program Manager who gets the word out in the disability community, walks families through an intake process, communicates with the camp, and schedules activities. We send a nurse from our team and hire part-time Child Care Specialists, but we partner with local churches to find volunteers we can train to staff the camp."

The beauty of this approach is that at least the Local Program Manager and the trained volunteers remain in their communities where they can encourage respite care through their local churches.

If partnering with a local camp sounds intriguing, your friends at Jill's House are happy to share what they've learned about the process. You'll find an in-depth guide to navigating the creation of a camp program beginning in Chapter 22.

Providing Holistic Family Support

Although much of the ministry of Jill's House revolves around providing overnight respite care, the vision of Jill's House is to support every member of families loving children with special needs.

So Jill's House has become creative in opportunities outside of overnight rest.

The Jill's House Family Support Team has created programs to address the needs of typically developing children who can feel overlooked and a little left behind when so much parental attention has to be directed at siblings with special needs.

And parents' need for friendship and social interaction is addressed through a Moms' book club during the school year and Dads' Nights Out at local restaurants throughout the year.

Occasional Friday night dinners during weekend check-ins provide an opportunity for parents to meet and encourage one another, and Summer Camp Coffees to do the same for parents dropping kids off for day camp.

Add to the list speaker seminars, workshops, and a retreat ministry—all avenues for Jill's House staff to truly know and love the families they serve... and to lay the foundation for evangelism and Christ-centered outreach.

Here's more detail about each of those approaches to encouraging holistic support and relationship.

Retreats

One of the most overtly evangelistic things Jill's House does is host retreats.

"We're now at the point where we do four retreats per year," said Dana. Like all of Jill's House programming, retreats started slowly, with just one. But the response was so positive, this out-of-the-building initiative just kept growing.

Family Retreats

A Jill's House Family Retreat is a weekend away where the entire family comes along—parents, children with special needs, typical children— everyone but the family pet.

"We take them out to the country to a retreat center and provide childcare for the entire weekend," said Dana. "We provide food, organize all the activities, and announce beforehand in our advertising that we'll have a speaker who'll be addressing issues that arise for families raising children with disabilities. We're clear from the beginning that the presenter will be speaking from the perspective of the Christian faith. We put that out there right up front."

Dana can recall receiving just one phone call from a concerned dad who wanted to know just *how* Christian the talks would be.

"I told him it would probably be pretty Christian but would also tackle challenges faced by families like his. He could take what he wanted from the talks and leave what he didn't want on the table," she said. "That family did end up attending, and they loved the experience."

So do other families who, at the retreat, experience something that happens nowhere else: Every other family looks like their family. Everyone they encounter understands the stresses they face.

Over the course of the weekend, as they realize they're in a safe place of honest acceptance, walls fall down and open and vulnerable conversations take place. And all in the context of the speaker's presentation of the Gospel message and the promise of true rest that message brings.

There's no need to apologize if a child has a meltdown or acts out in a way that would be bothersome elsewhere. There's room to run—or to sit quietly—whatever the children desire. And constantly there are smiling Jill's House staff and volunteers ready and willing to play, imagine, dress up, skip stones, or do whatever the kids want to do.

Jill's House staff and volunteers provide a wide range of accessible, family-friendly activities like hay rides, talent shows, and outdoor safari treasure hunts.

Tea parties for moms and hikes for dads build in rejuvenating "we're in this together" bonding with other parents and forge friendships that last far beyond the few days spent at the retreat.

Marriage Retreats

Jill's House hosts a marriage retreat where children don't attend—just their parents. Given that the stress of raising a child with profound disabilities can strain the strongest marriage, these weekends can literally save families.

"We take couples out for a few days, bring in a speaker, and let spouses focus on themselves and their relationships," said Joel.

Participants learn from one another and support one another during this retreat.

"One couple who went on our marriage retreat was actively planning a divorce. They were talking about how to divide assets and who would get the kids," Joel said. "The retreat set them on a new path, and two years later, their marriage is flourishing."

A Jill's House retreat won't save every marriage. But a retreat can carve out space for a couple to catch their breath and set a new trajectory, discover new skills, and, in the process, rediscover one another.

Single Moms Retreats

Nobody needs to experience an oasis of rest, renewal, and relationship more than a single mother raising a child with special needs on her own.

Jill's House hosts annual retreats for single mothers consisting of four days of activities for both moms and their children. Facilitated discussion helps moms connect with others who understand their lives and stretches of no-stress, quiet "me-time" gives moms the chance to unwind.

Moms have the chance to sit down with financial planning experts and pick through fashionable wardrobe accessories, donated by area businesses.

And few moms say "no" when Jill's House volunteers offer to clean out and wash their cars.

Meanwhile, kids are lavished with one-on-one attention from the Jill's House team, playing games, doing crafts, and taking part in epic silly-string parties.

Dads' Retreats

"Our dads' retreats grew out of a monthly dads' outing," said Mike Stralow, vice president of advancement at Jill's House. "Guys would get together for dinner and talk, and good things came out of that."

Mike wondered what would happen if the fathers of children with special needs could spend 24 hours together? What might happen then?

Fifteen dads joined Mike at a campground, and the experiment began around a campfire.

"We had all the right junk food," Mike said. "Marshmallows, hot dogs, sodas—nothing healthy in sight."

Men sat down around the fire at 7:00 p.m. on a Friday night and it wasn't until 11:30 p.m. that the last guys wandered off to find their bunks in the cabins. "Once they started talking, they kept talking," said Mike.

The next morning, the dads bonded over a high ropes course and zip line that ran for 800 feet. "These guys were whooping and hollering like teenagers," Mike laughed. It was a morning of backslapping, high fives, and encouragement.

The canoeing planned for the afternoon was put on hold when the dads came to Mike and suggested that, instead of splitting up, they stick together and hang out around a fire for more conversation.

As they were sharing stories, they became a community. They forged friendships. They realized they may be in different spots, but they were all in this fatherhood thing together.

Some say that getting a group of men—no matter who they are—to talk is next to impossible. That hasn't been Mike's experience. For his suggestions for how to design a Dads' Retreat see page 183.

Seminars

Occasionally, Jill's House hosts seminars featuring speakers who address specific issues of concern for families with special needs children. For instance, financial planning takes on an entirely new focus when a family has a special needs child.

If you've got a child who'll need care his or her entire life and who's likely to outlive you—how do you make sure that child is cared for? What sort of help is available from foundations and programs out there—places you might find help if only you knew who they were and how to reach them?

Brenda and Lon know what it is to feel concern about caring for a child with special needs.

"We hope Jill outlives us, but Jill needs great help to live. So we wonder: Who'll care for her when we're not here? Who'll love her, make sure she's clean, and be sure she's fulfilled?" Brenda said. "Jill needs a round-the-clock caregiver and right now we can provide that. But what happens when we're gone?"

In the Solomons' case, a younger couple they've known for more than ten years has agreed to move into the Solomons' house and care for Jill should something happen to Lon and Brenda.

Which—for the Solomons—is a huge answer to prayer.

But even with that plan in place, there are concerns. Will there be enough money? Is it invested properly to assure there's ongoing care for Jill? What paperwork, if any, needs to be completed to make a transition for Jill as easy as possible?

A qualified financial professional, one who's likely already nearby in your community that has experience serving families like the Solomons, can provide valuable insight to parents who have questions about the ongoing care of their children.

If your church will open its doors to host those sorts of seminars, providing respite care while parents network and find resources, it's a way to show you care about those parents as whole people, not just as consumers of respite care.

It sends a powerful message from your congregation to the disability community: We see you. We care about you. And we think that your joining with us would be a blessing to us.

For a list of the topics parents of children with disabilities report wanting to explore most, see Chapter 23.

And keep in mind that you can host a seminar almost anywhere: in your church building, at a local school, or a civic club. If your church doesn't own a facility, this is still something you can do—just schedule a room in your local library or town hall.

Nights of Worship

This year, for the first time, Jill's House began hosting a Family Night of Worship. Jill's House brings in a worship leader and sends invitations to every family on the Jill's House mailing list.

"We're saying, 'Most of you know we're a Christian organization and we do what we do for your families because Jesus loves us—and loves you, too. We want to gather with anyone who'd care to join us to spend some time worshipping together," said Dana. "Feel free to come and bring your children. If you're not a member of the Christian faith but you'd like to know more—you come, too. We'll explain who we are, and we'll all have dessert afterwards."

The response to the worship nights has been encouraging. Staff and families gather together in a relaxed and comfortable space. There are chairs, beanbags, and plenty of room for children to dance and twirl, or just walk to the music.

"There's something profound and holy when we're all gathered together as image-bearers of Christ praising him together," said Dana.

"The families who've attended seem hungry for a worship experience they can share with their children without being anxious that their children's worship might disrupt someone else's worship.

"There's a pervasive sense of acceptance and joy."

CHAPTER 10

MOVING FORWARD

*I*t's been said that any organization which is not growing is dying. There's no such thing as standing still, or no such thing as a time of reflection and rest.

That's why there's a Starbucks on every corner and McDonalds in over 100 countries.[4]

But is there really a need to hire an architect to add another hundred beds to Jill's House? For the Jill's House team to huddle around a map of North America, discussing ways to dot the map with Jill's House facilities from coast to coast?

Yes...and no.

There's a need for respite care spread all across that map, certainly.

"There are two and a half million families in this country we could be serving, and each year we serve about 600," said Joel. "Our vision for the future is one of growth. There's much more to do and far more people to serve."

So, yes, moving forward you can expect Jill's House to grow. It has to—the need is too great and their calling too heartfelt to ignore.

But Jill's House doesn't have to come to your community to serve, because you're already there. Your church already lives in your community. You're already ideally situated to do in your neighborhood what Jill's House does in theirs.

And your friends at Jill's House wouldn't deny you what you'll encounter as you launch a ministry of respite care.

The privilege of serving remarkable families whose appreciation for what you offer is deep and sincere.

---

4   McDonalds: https://friendlylocalguides.com/blog/story-first-mcdonalds-russia
     https://bridgetomoscow.com/curious-fact-moscow-mcdonalds
     https://en.wikipedia.org/wiki/McDonald%27s

The growth you'll experience as your congregation pulls together to truly see people who are too often overlooked, to open your doors to neighbors who will bring fresh gifts, talents, and perspective with them.

And the joy of shining Christ's love out into your community, only to see it reflected back in the faces of children who'll inspire you, bless you, and transform you.

Your friends at Jill's House wouldn't deny you that for anything—because they've learned how satisfying and rewarding it is to provide respite care.

So, yes, there's a need.

And, yes, Jill's House will meet all of it they can in any way they can.

And, yes, as you step up and step out to meet the need in your community, they'll always be just a phone call away. Ready to encourage you, guide you, and listen as you sort through how to get done everything you have to do.

"Consulting is something we're committed to providing," said Lon. "We'll help you see what you need to get started and then, when you've got those resources lined up, we'll talk again as often as you need to talk."

But your friends at Jill's House will do something else for you, too. Something far more important than dispensing advice.

They'll pray for you.

From the moment you first let them know you're looking to launch a respite ministry, straight through to the moment you open your doors for the first time to the children God will bring to you, they'll pray.

And when those first kids arrive, they'll celebrate along with you what God has done to make your ministry a reality.

Because they remember well what it's like the first time a family walks through the door.

Opening Night

October 2010: The team at Jill's House is ready. After so many years of planning and preparation, Jill's House is about to welcome its first overnight guests.

The lobby is spotless, every hallway freshly vacuumed. The fireplace is lilting away cheerfully, and the team is milling around the lobby, hardly believing that this moment has finally arrived.

And then it happens: A car pulls up outside the front entrance. The car doors swing open and a family steps out.

Tranitra was one of the team members eagerly waiting inside that evening.

"Our first night was so cool," she remembers. "We had six kids staying that weekend and there were probably 18 or 20 staff on hand to greet them. The CEO, the office staff, the folks who worked on the floor. We all wanted to be a part of that moment."

"It started with a half-dozen kids," added Dana. "But it wasn't long before we were at full capacity."

Within weeks, more and more parents pulled up out front. More families walked through those wide, welcoming doors into Jill's House. And more parents walked back outside to slide into their vehicles and a few days of desperately-needed respite.

Jill's House was no longer a dream.

It had become a home—one where rest, renewal, and love live.

NUTS, BOLTS, AND BEST PRACTICES

*W*hen McLean Bible Church started its special needs ministry, it wasn't difficult to find other churches who valued inclusive Sunday school classes. Getting some advice was as easy as picking up a phone and checking in with a few other congregations.

There were fewer models of how to create a Break Away or Breakout group, but suggestions about how to proceed were available if the ministry team looked.

But when it came to getting help with Jill's House—building a facility for overnight respite care that could address the needs of families raising children with profound intellectual disabilities—that was another story altogether.

"Jill's House didn't fit neatly into any existing model of respite care," said Dana. "There were in-home programs, summer camps, and after-school programs, but an overnight facility? That was a brand-new idea."

Which explains why finding Jerusalem's Shalva was such a boost to the team planning Jill's House. It provided an example of what was possible: outfitting and arranging bedrooms and bathrooms, creating common spaces, and picking appropriate programming. Everything from connecting with families, to feeding guests, to keeping track of medications—Jill's House representatives soaked it all in and brought the best of what they discovered back with them to northern Virginia.

After all, why reinvent something that's working? Better to adapt and tweak, taking advantage of the hard work already done by others.

Think of the remainder of this book as your trip to Jerusalem—your peek at what's working.

You've already seen what Jill's House has done and gotten a sense of who they are and why they do what they do. You know their heart for service.

And hopefully you've discovered this along the way: That heart for service includes serving *you* as you launch your respite care ministry.

That's the reason for this book: So you can catch the vision and then find the practical help you'll need to get started.

As you consider how to design your program, whether it's in a church building, at a camp, or out in your community, refer often to what's here. They're tips from the trenches—advice from your friends at Jill's House and others whose respite care ministries are further along than yours.

They're happy to share what they've learned with you and trust you'll be equally generous with other fledgling respite care ministries as they come to you for advice in the future.

Because we're all in this together—to the glory of God and the good of the Kingdom.

CHAPTER 11

GAINING APPROVAL
FOR A RESPITE CARE MINISTRY

*I*f you're part of a church and want to gain approval for launching your ministry, you probably won't have a Lon Solomon in your corner.

You'll be looking across the desk at a caring pastor who has a lot of other requests and proposals piled up on the desk already. Or at a leadership team that already has enough ministry to-dos to fund and administer to choke a reasonably healthy horse.

Even if you happen to *be* that caring pastor, sold on providing respite care, it's likely you'll have to make a case to a board that's well-aware the ministries of the church are stretched thin, and that new volunteers are rarer than unicorns.

Yet here you are, suggesting another program.

Your request for support—or at least permission to explore what it would take to create a respite care ministry—will be better received if you'll do the following:

- **Present a program you're willing to run, not a problem they need to solve**

  Very little happens until there's someone who owns it—and that includes new ministries in a church. Be clear that you're not coming to the pastor or board for funding or even manpower. You're coming to make certain that a respite care program aligns with the church's vision for ministry.

  Be clear about what you want to do—to provide respite for families raising children with disabilities as you care for those children—and the scope of your program. You're not out to simply be inclusive in your Sunday school program (something that's hopefully already happening) or to build another Jill's House.

You're after something in between—something like a monthly Saturday afternoon or a Friday night.

Explain where you are in the process: the beginning. You've not raised money, recruited volunteers, or put together an initial plan.

In fact, as you gather more information, you may decide that you're not the right person to carry this ministry forward. If that should be the case, you'll find the right person. But for now—it's you.

"That's an easy ask," said Denny. "You're not looking for a commitment; you're looking for alignment."

It's unlikely that any pastor or board will deny you permission to gather information about helping people in your community.

But don't settle for that, because that's only part of the story. Yes, there are families who are living with insufficient margin in their lives as they care for a child with special needs.

But there's another reason your church should move ahead with respite care, too, and you'll want to mention that at the outset: Because embracing a special needs ministry will do remarkable things for your church, too.

- **Have a clear, easy-to-articulate mission statement at the ready.**

We walk you through how to craft one beginning on page 159, and when asked to describe what you have in mind by a leader, it will be your answer.

The time to do what it takes to get your statement crisp and clear is *before* you go into a meeting, not when you're first asked.

- **Outline the benefits your church will experience if you host respite care**

It's easy to adopt an attitude of "Oh, these poor families are a mission project, but we don't necessarily expect them to actually become a part of our congregation."

It's true that many families served through your respite care will be outside your church. Some will be from outside the Christian faith. And many will never be back in your building for anything other than respite care.

But some will, and seeing them as a mission project sends a subtle, but insidious, message. It leaves families who are raising children with disabilities perpetually on the outside. Invited—sort of. Welcome—sort of.

Someone coping with cancer is no less able to contribute to the life and mission of the church than someone who's cancer-free. Someone in a wheelchair can give a testimony to God's faithfulness as well—or better—than someone who's sailed through life without challenges.

And a child who has a profound intellectual disability can radiate joy like a lighthouse.

Brenda can testify to what's to be learned from children with disabilities from her own experience with Jill.

"Jill is nonverbal now—her seizures have taken that ability away from her—but she's the best teacher I've ever had," said Brenda. "Her tenacity is amazing, and something neat about Jill is that she's no respecter of persons. She doesn't care if you have power or money. She'll grab the hand of a homeless man and show him love as quickly as she reaches out to someone who's wealthy or well-known. Jill has taught me so much about compassion and unconditional love. More than anyone else I know, she's living it out on a day-to-day basis."

Brenda continued, saying how children and adults with disabilities have so much to teach the rest of us that it behooves us to love, care for, and welcome them. "God sends them to us for a reason," Brenda said. "It may just be to show the rest of us how to love."

So, don't let your respite care ministry get off on the wrong foot. This isn't a project to solve a problem in the community that's somehow removed from your church.

It's a program to invite into your family new friends who'll bring with them something rich, valuable, and needed.

Your respite care program isn't posting a sign that help can be found if you'll wheel around back and knock on the kitchen door. You're laying out a welcome mat, front and center, with an invitation to come on in through the front door.

And if you sense disconnect between that attitude and what your leadership is thinking, mention these benefits that come to your congregation when you're hosting respite care.

Lon and Brenda Solomon with daughter Jill

FAMILY FUN IN A

Alex enjoying pool time with big brother Charlie at a weekend family retreat

Jacob showing off his sweet smile

RETREAT SETTING

Anbao loves canoeing at camp

Aiden and his family enjoying a weekend away at a family retreat

SOME FRIENDS AND MEMBERS

*Joni Eareckson Tada and her husband Ken
with the Solomons at Jill's House*

The Dharia family with Tim, a Jill's House caregiver

Waverly and Oliver McNeil relaxing

Katie Schmehl and her winsome smile

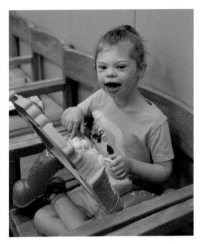

Blake enjoying some free time

Ava and her dad, Tae, sharing a hug

The Larson family enjoying a stroll

Adventure Heights provides a variety of activity options

McKenna and her caregiver Makenna spending one on one time together in Adventure Heights

One of the Pod Areas at Jill's House— bedrooms on the exterior & open play space in the middle

The Jill's House Pool: Shallow depth warm temperature, accessible entry, and chemical free treatment makes this a fan favorite

Arts & Crafts during a typical Sibling Night

JILL'S HOUSE

Big Sky Gym: The bounce house is a big hit with the kids

Ryan and his Jill's House caregiver Camilla in the Chapel

Rebecca exploring the Outdoor Playground with a Jill's House volunteer Mi Jin

One of the Sensory Rooms, providing a smaller and quieter environment for our guests

Thank you for coming with us on this journey of rest and relationship at Jill's House!

You'll be fulfilling the Great Commission

When Jesus sent his disciples out to tell the world about him and invite them into community, there wasn't an asterisk that added, "But only the able-bodied."

The parents drawn to your church through respite care will soon be asking what motivates you to provide this service to their children—and to themselves. That's an invitation to let them know you're passing along the love you've received from God—who loves his children just as desperately as those parents love their kids.

And that's the start of a conversation that leads to good places.

You'll be sharing God's love with your community

"Do you know who has benefited most from McLean Bible Church getting involved in respite ministry?" Lon poses the question and then answers it himself: "It's McLean Bible Church. Our providing respite care totally changed us. It gave us so much more compassion and transformed how we're viewed by the community around us. They came to see us as the kind of church we want to be—a church with a heart and soul to help."

You'll engage new people in ministry

In your congregation, there are people in the pews who care about respite care and the families you can serve. They're physical therapists, social workers, nurses, special education teachers, and people who grew up alongside a sibling or friend who had special needs.

"Those people aren't serving in respite care because nobody has made a way for them to do it," said Lon. "Until church leadership opens up the possibility, they'll just sit there."

A respite care ministry sparks the interest of those people and speaks to what they already find important. They're far likelier to pull themselves off the pew and dive into ministry to do something they see as needed than to take on another task that doesn't seem as vitally important.

Your team won't deplete the ranks of Sunday school teachers. Instead, it will draw new volunteers into service.

You'll embrace inclusion and service

Anyone under 40 years old has been raised in a world where inclusion is a matter of course—and serving others is viewed so favorably that service hours can be required for high school graduation.

So have a place that people can serve—not just by going on occasional international mission trips or once a year on a church-wide campaign but regularly.

Respite care signals that you care. That you're all-in for selflessly serving the local community. That you're fully participating in the world around you.

It's where you give young people a chance to make a difference.

You'll draw new families into your church

Not a flood of families and probably not right away. But they'll come—and when they come, they'll have much to teach you.

They'll show you what commitment looks like and what serving one another looks like.

What compassion looks like when it's lived out day after day, night after night, for years on end.

And there's this: It will quickly dawn on you that among the greatest blessings for which you're thankful are these families who are teaching you to love in new, Jesus-like ways.

You'll forge lifelong relationships

Dana remembers being invited to the graduation party a family held when their daughter with special needs aged out of the school system.

"At the party were friends from the neighborhood where the family had once lived, friends from their current neighborhood, and family that came in from near and far," Dana said. "And then there was me."

Dana had been asked to say a few words to help celebrate the moment. She noticed next to a screen where a slideshow of the young woman's life was showing, sat a binder filled with familiar paperwork.

"When a child stays at Jill's House, we send home a *My Stay* form describing what the child did each day. It shares what the child enjoyed, who played with the child, and wraps up by identifying the primary caregiver as 'the staff member who was blessed to care for your child,'" said Dana. "Those forms—all of them from every visit—were carefully catalogued in the binder."

The parents told Dana those forms were the only positive feedback they'd ever received about their daughter.

"Schools documented everywhere their girl missed the mark," said Dana. "Doctors, social workers, and physical therapists listed all the developmental markers their daughter hadn't hit. But at Jill's House we didn't judge their child. We *celebrated* her—and that made a huge difference to those parents. We'll be friends forever."

CHAPTER 12

COMMUNICATING WITH YOUR CONGREGATION

Sometimes in the church, we take that whole "don't let your left hand know what your right hand is doing" (Matthew 6:3) passage out of context.

Jesus was talking about humility in giving, not failing to mention to the women's Bible study group that the Cub Scouts are scheduled to use the fellowship hall for a dodge ball tournament the same morning the ladies plan to have a prayer meeting.

When we don't communicate clearly, it needlessly complicates life.

As you begin planning your respite ministry, do so knowing there are key audiences you need to keep in the loop. People you want informed, and not just when you're ready to launch.

The first audience is your congregation. And coming right behind it is another: the community at large.

Communicating with your congregation

- **From the pulpit**
  If you have a church of 30, the best way to let people know what you're up to is in person. Ask for five minutes to share what's happening at a worship service and then take four minutes to communicate the following:

  - What respite is and why it's needed in your community. A quick statistic is fine, but a description of what life is like for a typical family you're intending to serve is more compelling. Consider sharing Tricia's story, the one you'll find on page 26, or better yet, have a family within the congregation with a child who has special needs speak to the need for belonging and rest.

- What embracing families who are raising children with special needs will do for your congregation: You'll share God's love as you shine it into your community, draw new families into your church's circle of influence and perhaps into your fellowship, serve your neighbors in a meaningful way, and be inspired by remarkable families.
- Where you are in the planning process.
- Invite anyone who feels called to know more to catch you for a further conversation. Avoid taking any questions from the floor—this isn't the time or place—and it's unlikely you're ready with the details someone will want.
- Invite everyone to consider who among their neighbors might benefit from this ministry when it's launched. This is key—it will immediately make relevant your ministry to anyone who knows a family raising a child with special needs.

Don't give too much detail. You won't *have* much at the outset and providing a detailed briefing isn't your goal.

You're simply sharing a vision and casting a wide net for people who might want to join you in shaping your congregation's respite program.

Please note: Asking for five minutes and taking just four is strategic.

You'll want to give periodic updates as the project revs up and moves into high gear. If you ramble on past your allotted time the first opportunity you have to present the ministry, you won't be getting behind the microphone again.

So, practice—a dozen times, if necessary—until you can nail your briefing within the time you've been given to share it.

As the congregation hears about how the ministry is coming along, it will slowly come to be seen not as just *your* mission, but *our* mission. That's essential when the time comes to request funding or designated space.

There are two additional reasons for talking congregation-wide about the respite program.

First, doing so gives everyone a common language for sharing *what* you're doing and *why* you're doing it.

Here's what you *don't* want: A member of your congregation with good intentions, but little interaction with the disability community, shares with the parent of a child with special needs that his church is starting a respite program for "retarded kids, like little Jonathan there."

That's one family who will never darken the door of your respite program.

A second reason is for keeping people posted. As you update the congregation, you're also updating the church leadership. And if the leaders value the new ministry, you'll find that doors open for you.

If your congregation is larger or you're spearheading a program that includes volunteers from more than one church, ongoing communication becomes even more important. The opportunity for being misunderstood or lost in the shuffle magnifies, and you'll want to communicate in writing as well as verbally.

So we've provided some sample text for church bulletins, mailings, emails, and website announcements.

• **Communicating through church bulletin and emails**

Yes, there are churches that still distribute bulletins as congregants enter worship services. Yours might be among them.

If that's the case, you know that bulletins actually get read, most often during extended musical solos and sermons.

And if your church has an email list that you can use to reach members and visitors, that's a great way to communicate about your respite ministry as well.

Keep in mind your emails live and die based on the subject line. Add a few too many exclamation points or be too coy about who's writing, and your message will be picked off by the spam filter or land in the trash.

Avoid that by being clear about who's writing and why.

And, if possible, promise a benefit if someone will open your email and read it.

Following are some sample emails that can be adapted for use by your church. Adapt the text to serve as announcements in bulletins, too.

An email for when your ministry is just forming...

At this stage you're not recruiting volunteers. You're letting everyone know what you're planning to do and seeing who might like to help you.

Remember: You don't know who grew up with a sibling who had special needs, who is especially sensitive to this need in your community, or who God might be calling to come alongside you.

It's not likely you'll get a large response—but even one person who'll bring expertise and enthusiasm is something to celebrate.

Subject   **How First Christian Church's new ministry will open your eyes to the love of God in a new way...**

First Christian's new respite care program is for you...

- **If you're the parent of a child with special needs**, you'll be able to have a few hours each week of rest and renewal.
- **If you aren't raising a child with special needs**, serving in this ministry will help you grow in your faith in amazing ways. Plus, you'll help First Christian shine the love of God into our community.

We're talking now about how to shape this ministry. We'd welcome the insights of anyone with a heart for families raising children with special needs, for children, and for serving our community. If that's you, please call **Jill Jackson at 555-5555** for a quick chat.

We'd love to share with you what we're planning and hear what you think!

An email for when your ministry is looking for volunteers...

Once again, blasting out an announcement that you're seeking volunteers is something you do after carefully selecting people you believe are wired for respite ministry.

But after you've plucked the fruit you most want, it's time to shake the tree and see if you missed someone God might be calling to serve with you.

That can be done in an email, but be aware that open rates are often—at best—abysmal. You can expect roughly 25% of your recipients to open your email and fewer to carefully read it.

But if you net one or two qualified and committed volunteers, it's well worth the effort...especially since you can adapt this text:

Subject   From First Christian: Is this God calling?

First Christian's new Respite Care Ministry is moving along.
We've got a newly-decorated space, a clear calling from God to serve our community by giving parents raising children with special needs a few hours of rest and renewal, and we're counting down to our Grand Opening.
Now it's time for you to ask: Is God nudging you to help?
It's not a life-long commitment or even a large one. But it *is* important—and well worth your time.
You may be exactly the right person for this ministry if you...

- **Can set aside one Friday night per month between the hours of 5:00 and 10:00 p.m.** That's when we'll be caring for children in the Fellowship Hall.
- **Love kids and can play with them.** We want this to be a super experience for children and will have crafts, creative movement, music, games, and videos available. If you're willing to buddy up with one or two children for these activities, this may be for you.
- **Want to shine God's love into our community.** We've checked—respite care is what parents raising kids with special needs say is in desperately short supply, and we're stepping up to provide it. We're loving our neighbors in a practical way.
- **Love to have fun.** You'll be with some of the most spectacular people you'll ever meet as you serve these children. And you'll be supporting parents who love their kids with a passion that's inspirational. Friday night respite care shifts will be the high point of your month.
- **Can pass a background check.** We all have a past, and yours may include some things you're happy are behind you. But we'll ask—we have to so we can tell parents we're providing the safest environment possible for their children. Some things on

a background check won't matter, some will. But know that we'll be needing you to take one.

If you think serving may be for you, let's talk about it. Call the church office at (555) 555-5555 and we'll connect you with the ministry team for a chat.

An email announcing your Grand Opening…

Subject   You're invited to the Grand Opening. Bring a smile!

We're excited—and you're invited!

First Christian's Respite Care Grand Opening and Prayer Dedication is Friday evening, (month) (day) between (time) and (time)…and we want you there.

Please come tour the room and equipment children will use as they buddy up with volunteers. Pray with us as we thank God for this chance to serve our community.

And have cake!

This is an open house—you're welcome any time between (time) and (time).

We won't be providing childcare this evening, but we encourage you to bring your kids. We love them—and you!

First Christian Respite Care Team
First Christian Church
123 Oak Street
Your town, Ohio 45223
firstchn/respite.org
(555) 555-5555

CHAPTER 13

COMMUNICATING WITH YOUR COMMUNITY

*M*cLean Bible Church and Jill's House discovered something that seems counter-intuitive: As long as parents have waited for respite care, as much as they desire it, they're sometimes...slow...to take advantage of it.

Or maybe "cautious" is a better word.

"Parents raising children with special needs live with fears," said Brenda. "They have fears about the future, fears for their children's health, and fears for themselves."

So those parents quickly become very careful about who and what they trust with their children. Your hanging out a shingle that said, "Respite care provided here," doesn't mean they'll automatically assume you know what you're doing.

Because those same parents also grow accustomed to living with disappointments, Brenda added.

Programs make promises that aren't kept. Optimistic therapists predict outcomes that never happen. Employers, who once accommodated unpredictable schedules grow weary of making adjustments.

It feels that life is primed and ready to toss one disappointment after another at parents who often learn to lower their expectations.

So it's just natural that the respite care you offer looks too good to be true. They may approach you cautiously, with as many questions for you as you have for them.

Don't be offended. They're doing the due diligence they should do.

They're protecting their children.

What will increase participation from families like nothing else is word-of-mouth endorsements from families who've used your services. But like all new enterprises, your ministry can't get those until you've had people show up.

What to do?

As already mentioned, network with agencies and organizations those families already trust. Reach out personally. Pick up the phone. Invite parents to check you out.

And add to that a strategy to reach out with inexpensive advertising courtesy of...your humble church bulletin.

Adding a well-designed bulletin insert that congregants can carry home with them to pass to a neighbor or friend, or to post in the community, deputizes your entire congregation to market your ministry.

But be sure to include inserts at least three weeks in a row. It's not unusual for congregants to come to worship services just two or three times per month.

Creating a bulletin insert mini-poster

This isn't a place to skimp on design.

Your mini-poster will end up on workplace or social club bulletin boards, displayed at other churches, and taped up next to larger posters in a neighborhood business. You need it to be clear, crisp, and easy to read.

From the pulpit, announce you're deputizing anyone holding a bulletin to take home the insert and post it someplace families in the community will see it.

Even better, if there's a neighbor or family friend who's raising a child with special needs, the insert can be delivered personally.

Announce a downloadable electronic version is available at your church website and invite congregants to link to and repost it wherever they'd like.

Some people who see your mini-poster won't know what "Respite Care" means, but those who most need it will know exactly what's being offered—and welcome the invitation.

Because mini-posters will be distributed broadly, be careful about what contact information you provide. It would be more personal to list a name and cell phone number, but think twice before doing that. Filtering calls through a church office during business hours and returning those calls promptly is the safest way to go.

Here's text to get you started:

RESPITE CARE AVAILABLE

Friday Evenings, 6p.m. – 10p.m.

This Friday evening, enjoy precious hours of rest and renewal as we care for your child with special needs.

Our trained volunteers will give your child a fun evening of games, crafts, sing-alongs, new friends, and undivided attention while you catch your breath.

A nurse will be on duty.

Call our office at (555) 555-5555 for more information and to reserve a spot for your child.

First Christian Respite Care Team
First Christian Church
123 Oak Street
Your town, Ohio 45223
firstchn/respite.org
[END OF BULLETIN INSERT]

Online advertising

First, know this: It can be intimidating to venture into the world of pixels, layouts, and online advertising. If that's not something you're familiar with, ask around in your congregation to see if someone who's more adept at this skill and is willing to volunteer some time to create and maintain a site for you.

Or default to simply firing up a fresh Facebook page sharing your story.

But do give this consideration. Many people, when seeking anything in your community, start by doing an online web search—if you're not there, you won't hear from those people.

So, if you're not a web guru, you don't necessarily have to do any of what follows. But if you know a web guru, here's something you can pass along with a request to make it happen.

Let's start with two assumptions: You're not a mega-church, so the number of hits your website receives per week is minimal.

And you don't have a professional web designer standing by to help you get a respite care ministry site up and running. Perhaps you paid one to set up your church website, but that was a long time ago.

And you certainly don't feel like learning to design and maintain websites yourself.

Yet you need a landing page at your church website that has information about your respite care ministry. People in the community who hear about you need a place to get additional information.

They want to know the scope of what you do. They want to see some photos of where children spend time, get a peek at your policies and procedures, find out about fees, and they may want to send you a quick email to get some questions answered.

Your website is also a place potential volunteers can discover what opportunities are available to them.

Your web presence doesn't have to be complicated—it shouldn't be, in fact—but your website *does* have to exist. And it needs to exist before you launch any marketing so you can include the location on all outgoing communication.

Given your ministry and community-service focus, don't immediately offer to pay someone for design help. Some professionals do pro-bono work for select nonprofits. Ask around.

Also contact your local community college or high school and talk with whoever is teaching website design. Explain you're launching a respite care program, and you don't have funds, but you have a real-world project you'd love to have the class tackle either for free or a reduced rate.

You'll be stunned how often a college professor or high school teacher will ask an especially promising student if he or she wants to get some real-life experience.

When you meet with your web guru, be it someone you're paying or who is working for free, give the following guidance:

- **Keep it simple.** Easy to navigate, easy to read, easy to link to the Respite Care Ministry page from the church website. If your respite care website is crowded, busy, or packed with the latest online wizardry, it communicates exactly the *opposite* of "restful." You're aiming for clean, concise, and professional.

  For a stellar example, visit our Jill's House friends at Jillshouse.org for inspiration. They've done it right.

- **Use high-quality graphics and images, but only sparingly.** And no photos showing children without having written permission from parents.

  That said, *do* get permission to use photos of children with special needs. It's absolutely worth the effort.

  "When parents of special needs kids look at your website and see a child in a wheelchair or wearing headphones and looking at an iPad, that parent will think, 'Oh, they can work with me and my child.'" said Shannon, a parent in northern Virginia. "Even if other parents don't notice, parents like me are looking for any visuals or verbiage that lets us know our kids are welcome."

- **Be sure your webpage works with phones, tablets, and other devices.** Few people will find you while seated at a desktop computer or laptop.

- **Include this information:** A brief welcome statement, a description of who you serve, and why you serve. If you charge for respite care, say so. Provide an address and contact information that allows for sending email directly from your page.

- **Think twice about having people fill out intake forms online.** At Jill's House that's possible, but they've put firewalls in place and have the know-how to manage the sensitive information provided. Unless you're certain you have the proper procedures in place and someone will be monitoring the site daily, don't collect electronic data.

- **As soon as you have testimonials from families, include them.** Always with permission and, if possible, with a photo.

- **Have your website builder provide training for *maintaining* the site.** You'll want to swap out copy and add and delete event information.

- **If you're getting pro bono help from a student, pay something anyway.** If it's a gift card to a coffee shop, load it up with enough money to keep the kid caffeinated through the rest of the semester. The work that was done is worth it.

Check out neighborhood online groups. They come and go, but there's always at least one site that lets neighbors post information about garage sales, free stuff, and stray dogs.

Place an ad for your respite care ministry there, too—in as many nearby neighborhoods as possible.

Search out the websites of relevant agencies and organizations, too. Connect with your local Arc chapter, Parents of Autistic Children or Down syndrome group, and other advocacy or support groups. See if they're willing to link to your website, possibly with an endorsement attached. Local closed Facebook groups that connect parents of special needs children will be hungry to hear what you're doing—send a request and then offer to provide information.

Issue press releases

What you're doing is newsworthy—it's unusual, community-minded, needed, and your local news outlets may well cover it if you let them know about it.

And don't just think about the big daily paper in town. You'll also want to contact neighborhood weekly or monthly publications.

Any news outlet that cares about your community needs a personal invitation to your Grand Opening—and encourage print media to send a photographer along as well. If you expect reporters to show up, have a list of talking points ready for your interview.

And if there's a parent of a special needs child who's served on your team, do whatever it takes to have that person on hand and prepared for interviews. That parent will be able to explain the need for your ministry in ways that no amount of statistics will communicate.

It's easy to write a press release, but it gets harder as you re-write it. And you *will* re-write it—probably several times. You'll need to keep whittling away what doesn't need to be there. Bump up the "hook" that grabs a reporter's attention. Shorten and simplify.

Here's a step-by-step guide to writing that press release that will announce your ministry to your community:

- **Craft a clear, compelling headline** that engages the reader while still explaining what you're writing about. This isn't a place to be shy or clever. Write your headline in **bold type**, and *italicize* the subhead if you include one.

- **Be concise.** The reporter who's reading your press release will give you about 10 seconds to convince her that your story is more worthy of coverage than the other ten press releases littering her inbox. Reporters and editors are busy, so don't make them wade through endless paragraphs to get to your point.

- **Signal you're local** by including a dateline indicating your city and when you released the press release. You want your local paper to immediately realize that this is a local story, of interest to their local subscribers.

- **Include a quote from someone on your team.** Or better, from a parent of a child with special needs. A quote from someone local gives your press release more relevance and personality.

- **Give the facts of your respite program, but don't coat them in dust.** The who, what, when, where, and why details don't need to be dry, but get to them quickly.

- **Add "boilerplate" copy.** This is the same stuff you'd put in the "About Us" section of your website. It's basic background that gives the reporter enough to describe your organization without having to do a lot of digging.

- **Check your work for typos and poor grammar.** Because if you don't, you'll undermine your credibility.

- **Quick-response contact information.** Reporters work on tight deadlines, so have a name and cell phone number that can be reached quickly and easily. Better yet, identify two people who can handle the calls and list them both.

[THE NAME
OF THE CHURCH]

Sample Press Release

For Immediate Release

Contact:
Jenny Smith (555) 555-5555
j.smith@mail.com

Sam Johnson (555)555-5555
sam@mail.com

LOCAL CHURCH OFFERS FREE RESPITE CARE FOR FAMILIES RAISING CHILDREN WITH SPECIAL NEEDS
First Christian Church hosts Friday evening respite sessions beginning this week

[YOURTOWN, YOUR STATE] First Christian Church will host a weekly respite session for families raising children with special needs beginning this Friday. The church will accept up to 20 children for the 5:00 p.m. to 10:00 p.m. session and families are invited to apply by calling (555) 555-5555.

"Trained volunteers will provide care for the children," said First Christian's Respite Ministry Coordinator Jenny Smith. "We will also have a nurse on site."

Applicants do not need to be church members, but they do need to complete an application form providing contact and medical information. Children who attend will take part in crafts, enjoy snacks and music, and be led in active play.

"We want this to be an enjoyable time for kids and a restful time for parents," said Smith. The church has converted several rooms to make them accessible and to provide a space for children's activities.

Smith expects slots to fill quickly and encourages parents to call promptly to schedule one of the Friday evening sessions.

"We've been planning this for two years," said First Christian's Smith. "We're eager to serve area families in this way."

About First Christian Church
First Christian Church, a non-denominational church located at 1414 Samson Lane, has been a part of the [Yourtown] community since 1994. Its mission is to love and serve God and to love and serve others. The church's respite care ministry was launched in response to what church members see as a need in the community for easily-accessible, caring, free respite care.

Don't forget letters to the editor
Even if a reporter doesn't cover your Grand Opening or the launch of your ministry, you can still get press.

And get it on a page that's often one of the most closely read in a typical paper: the editorial section.

Do this: Ask someone who has benefited from your services to write a brief letter about your ministry. Have them describe what you do and the impact having respite sessions has had on the writer's family.

Let it be a letter of thanks—and a call for more organizations to step up and provide similar care.

No, it's not a page one story—but you're still getting the message out.

CHAPTER 14

AMERICANS WITH DISABILITIES ACT

$\mathcal{B}$e mindful that your entire building doesn't need to be ADA compliant to launch a respite care ministry. If your church was designed after 1990 and happens to sit in the United States, it's probably already largely compliant.

But if your church meets in a stately old 1909 brick building that would require demolition to begin making it compliant, don't despair.

First, while churches are required to comply with portions of the ADA, they're exempt when it comes to public accommodation—like your respite care program. If you want to confirm that, refer to Title 111, Section 3.102(e) of the ADA for specifics.

That said, why wouldn't you *want* to be as compliant as possible? To open up as much of your facility as possible to people of all abilities? Welcoming them into your community includes welcoming them into your public assemblies and worship services.

But if full ADA compliance isn't a possibility, do this: Pick a few rooms that are compliant, or can easily be made compliant, and let that be your respite ministry area. You'll be limited as to the number of children you can serve at one time, but that's also true of Jill's House. It's true of any building.

The United States government provides an 89-page checklist you can find online (adachecklist.org/doc/fullchecklist/ada-checklist.pdf) to see how your respite area stacks up, but you don't need to go to that level of detail. You may need to make some modifications, but some are relatively easy to do and aren't expensive. If you have specific questions call the ADA Information Line at 800-514-0301.

We've provided a starter checklist (you're welcome!) in an appendix at the end of this book. Walk around your respite care area with the list in hand and see what you might be able to do to make your space as welcoming—and obstacle-free—as possible.

CHAPTER 15

THE ART OF FIGURING OUT FUNDING

*J*f you'll only need a few dollars to buy craft supplies, you're not likely to need to engage in fund raising.

But if, like some churches that choose to revamp and outfit a dedicated space for a respite care ministry, or who discover that there's a significant amount of work to do to make space ADA compliant, you have to raise some money. Here are some tips to get you started.

1. Start by talking with people who care about what you care about

They're out there—and they're often remarkably helpful.

Your local Arc chapter, county and community agencies, and school system professionals who engage with and support children with disabilities are all potential sources of valuable information.

They may not give you funds, but they'll connect you with people who could.

Keep in mind that anyone who works with families who have children with special needs is aware of the desperate need for respite care. These agencies and individuals will likely be sympathetic to your cause, even if you're operating in a faith-based place like a church building.

The truth is that you're *doing* something—and that alone will earn you a meeting and a listening ear.

But if you expect cooperation or referrals, be clear you're welcoming all people who meet the parameters of your program—not just church members. Be equally clear your heart is to serve without expectation; this isn't a thinly-veiled evangelism program designed to make converts.

You can ask families who have special needs children to make donations, but those families are often strapped for cash, said Denny. What they *can* offer is an introduction to organizations you might not know about.

"Networking is important," said Denny, who sometimes found support and financing followed someone's heartfelt appeal to a circle of friends. "What's key is not just getting to interested people you know, but through them, to interested people you've not yet met. When you make connections, keep track of them and be sure to develop them."

Social media plays a vital role, so find someone who'll own getting the word out via a variety of platforms. Just make sure that everyone is on the same page about what the message is—confusion quickly undermines your credibility.

Who cares about resourcing families in your community (and county and state) that have children with special needs? They'll care about respite—and need to know what you'll do to provide respite.

2. Ask your church to set up a designated fund in the church budget

Check with your church leadership about how to create a fund that can't be diverted away from your respite care ministry to other places. Arranging a way for people to donate through your church makes their gifts tax-deductible and allows you to tell businesses that want to donate money that you're a recognized non-profit.

Make it easy to donate to the fund, too. If your church has an online giving option, have whoever works on the website create a separate button for giving to your respite care effort.

And do your due diligence: Ask the church accountant to show you how he or she is keeping your monies separate from other church funds.

3. Stretch precious dollars by asking for discounts and in-kind giving.

"When it came time to build, we went after discounts and in-kind contributions from vendors," said Denny. "At minimum, we explained respite care and what we were doing and asked if we were getting the absolute best price. It's amazing how often the price dropped."

The point isn't to guilt a carpet store into cutting you a deal. It's to help store owners see that they, too, can be part of making respite care available in your community.

"You never know who has a child, brother, or a friend with special needs and this effort touches their hearts," said Denny.

Those are people who are happy to work with you on a discount because they value what you value. They know the need and see the benefit.

So, don't be shy about asking. The worst they can say is "no."

4. Host galas and other events…maybe

Jill's House has hosted its share of galas and events—and then some. And some of those events have brought in significant money that arrived at absolutely critical moments, keeping forward momentum alive.

But occasionally those events cost nearly as much money to pull off as they raised. And a break-even fundraiser isn't much of a fundraiser.

"There was a silver lining," Denny remembers. "Sometimes events brought people to Jill's House who could then be approached later about donating money. They were receptive because they'd heard our story at the gala or concert. None of those events were wasted effort and we appreciated them all."

Well…almost all.

Some events created significant headaches because when they were about to happen, it became clear wheels had fallen off along the way. A sound system hadn't been reserved or the catering confirmed. Details had fallen through the cracks.

"That meant we had to pull staff off other projects to get everything done," said Denny. Fundraising is important, but so is getting information to a planning commission or networking with agencies.

"It got to the point that, when someone wanted to do a fundraiser for us, we'd say, 'We'd love for you to do that, but we can't help make it happen. We just don't have the time.'"

Denny chuckled as he remembered some of those conversations. "I had to figure out a way to say, 'We'll do whatever we can to help—so long as you don't need our help.'"

One fundraiser where wheels have not only stayed on, but keep rolling along year after year, is a motorcycle ride that sends hundreds of bikes thundering through northern Virginia, with the ride ending at Jill's House for lunch and a tour.

"The organization handles everything," said Denny. "They provide needed funds while still freeing up Jill's House staff to work on other things."

As you consider fundraising events to raise money for your respite care ministry, count the costs—*all* the costs. What will the effort require of you in terms of time, effort, investment, focus, and opportunity cost? What will you need to give up doing to pull off the event?

Golf outings, silent auctions, 5ks, and concerts are wonderful—but they're *especially* wonderful if taken on by people who won't ask you to do most of the work.

5. Contact foundations for grants, but know it can be a long, frustrating process

There are foundations with money to donate, but the process of application and grant writing can be tedious—and the outcome uncertain. Foundations often receive far more requests than they can fund, so even if their funding goals align closely with your respite care program, they may not come through for you.

Or they may choose not to fund you because you don't quite fit what they're looking to fund. Yes, they care about families with special needs, but they only fund transportation to and from appointments, or medical equipment, or counseling.

Jill's House discovered that some foundations that work with special needs families hesitated when they realized Jill's House has a spiritual component.

"We had to be very, very clear that we work with families regardless of their faith, or lack of faith," said Denny. So, if you intend to apply for grants and have a similar stance regarding faith, take a page from the Jill's House playbook and lead with that information. Say it clearly and way up front.

An alternative to approaching national or regional foundations is to call on major companies in your immediate area. Many have charitable budgets as part of their giving back to the local community.

"Because you're a resource to the local community, you'll likely be able to get a meeting," said Denny. "Sit down with someone and find out the company's giving practices and how you can go about asking for a donation."

But before approaching companies, have your financial ducks in a row. Companies will want to be sure you're a credible organization and may be hesitant to donate directly to a church. Here's where having your church have a designated fund in place will prove useful.

"Don't be afraid to ask people in your network who work at companies to get information and make introductions," said Denny. "And if your request for money is denied, get feedback. Politely ask if there's anything you could or should do to be considered in the future."

6. Be careful about accepting money that comes with strings attached

Jill's House found itself in a position that looked like an answer to prayer.

Early on in the building process, when construction couldn't continue without a sizable influx of cash, a congressman from the district was able to earmark federal funds for specific phases of the building project.

Denny recalled that the initial reaction of the Jill's House boosters was elation. "It was a lot of money and it just sat there, waiting for us to claim it," he said.

But then the team paused to think through the implications of accepting the cash. "We had to ask how likely it was that, if we used the funds, we'd later be told we had to modify our hiring practices," he said.

It had been assumed that, as an integrated auxiliary of McLean Bible Church, Christians would be hired to fill positions at Jill's House. After all, Jill's House was a ministry—and the church had leeway to hire believers for ministry positions.

But if the facility was partially built with federal dollars, might that become a problem?

"In the end we didn't claim the money," said Denny. "We told the government we wouldn't apply for the funds."

If you accept donations for your respite care ministry, be equally diligent about not taking money from organizations or individuals that might expect something in return.

A seat on your board, perhaps, or an expectation that a sizable donation allows someone to set policy.

Gifts must come without strings attached, warned Denny. If you suspect otherwise, don't cash the check.

7. Decide: Will you charge for providing care?

Granted, Jill's House has expenses that a Saturday afternoon, church-based respite care program won't have. A mortgage and paid staff, for instance.

So, Jill's House has a rate structure for providing care—a rate that doesn't begin to cover all the related expenses. And a structure that doesn't keep any family from taking part in the respite program.

A sliding scale provides room for families with means to contribute to the ministry—and they're often happy to do so—while not creating a barrier for families unable to pay.

Remember that you're providing a service that's valuable to families. They'll gladly pay the going rate for a babysitter, especially since the care provided by your ministry includes activities for their child rather than simply oversight as the child interacts with a tablet.

If you're uncomfortable discussing money in the context of ministry, simply make your services free. Always. For everyone.

But do be willing to accept donations.

CHAPTER 16

RESPONDING TO FEARS ABOUT LAUNCHING A RESPITE CARE MINISTRY

*N*othing can derail ministry like fear.

Fears cause church leaders to circle the wagons around existing programs, avoiding the risk of trying something new and perhaps failing.

Which means fears can get in the way of launching a respite care ministry.

Though, according to Jill's House President Joel Dillon, fears might not really be the issue.

"I don't think it's necessarily fear that keeps a church from having a special needs ministry or providing respite care," he said. "I think it's that pastors aren't aware of the simple things they could do that would make their congregations more welcoming of the families they could be serving."

Fair point. Families raising children with special needs don't always come knocking on church doors looking to be welcomed there. So, it's not that pastors are deliberately ignoring the need for respite care; they simply don't see it.

But once church leaders are aware of the need and are deciding whether to green-light a respite care ministry, fears sometimes do come into play.

And Jill's House is all too happy to help put those fears to rest.

"There's not a week that goes by that someone doesn't contact us to pick our brain about our program," said Joel. "We do a lot of informal consulting about how to get started and move forward. We're happy to do it; it's one way we can have an impact. If nothing else, we let people learn from the mistakes we've made along the way."

The following are fears that have arisen as churches considered respite care ministries. Don't let any of them become deal breakers as you talk with your leaders.

"What about liability?"

As Virginia O'Connell has pointed out, you can provide the same level of medical care that a school typically provides. And if a child is so medically fragile that you can't provide adequate care, it's within your power to respectfully not include that child in your respite care program. "No" in this case is a loving word.

If what's behind this fear is concern about a lawsuit, do the following:

- Ask your church's attorney if offering to provide volunteer-led respite care crosses any line about overpromising the level of care that can be expected. It doesn't—you aren't claiming to be a medical facility, and you'll be clear that children will be cared for by non-medically certified volunteers.

- And while your attorney or the church board has the paperwork at hand, have them review the church's general liability insurance. It's likely you have coverage for when a Vacation Bible School program invites neighborhood kids onto the property, or the youth group goes on a mission trip. Hosting respite care will likely fall into the same general category—but make sure.

- Ask the church leadership if other vulnerable populations might also need to be excluded. The elderly, for instance, or perhaps infants. Both are on the edges of any bell curve describing vim and vigor.

- Distribute copies of the intake form and release form (in Chapter 17). Demonstrate that you're serious about limiting liability.

- Request that, if permission is granted to move the ministry forward, the forms you'll be using be forwarded to the church's attorney for vetting. In fact, when the time comes, *insist* on it.

"Where's the doctor?"

You don't need one. It's that simple. Virginia provides everything you'll need to dispel this fear in Chapter 7.

Though take this opportunity to probe a bit: Is there any particular reason this fear has surfaced? Has someone on the leadership team dealt with a situation where inadequate medical care resulted in a tragedy?

Two reasons to pause here: First, fears often are irrational by nature. Someone who encountered severe turbulence during a flight may experience heart palpitations on every flight afterwards for years. If someone on your elder board, session, or pastoral committee has experienced a tragedy because adequate medical care was unavailable, that will color how your ministry is viewed. Explore any fears, so you can put risk into perspective.

"What if we can't find enough volunteers?"

Be clear this concern is one you'll own. Reassure leaders that since safety is a concern, and you'll maintain a volunteer to child ratio, the ministry will never lack for volunteers.

If you're able to find two volunteers, you'll limit participation to the number of children two volunteers can handle. If you have a dozen volunteers, you'll open up participation to that level.

Under this fear is sometimes a concern that a new ministry will siphon off volunteers who are currently serving in other ministries. And while that may happen, assure leaders you'll also draw in new volunteers who aren't currently feeling called to existing ministries.

"Why bother with respite care when there's nobody here who needs it? We're creating a program to meet a need we don't have."

That no families raising children with special needs are coming to church isn't a sign that there are no families in that situation. It's an indication that they don't find any programming at your church sufficiently welcoming and compelling to prompt them to come.

Once you create programming and let them know, you'll see families come.

And should anyone wonder if there are enough families out there to warrant creating a ministry for them, do this: Call your local school district and ask how many children are receiving some sort of special education.

Numbers vary by district, but don't be surprised to learn that about 12% of kids in the district qualify for special education services.

If there were 12% of the families in your neighborhood starving, would there be any question that creating a food pantry was a good idea?

"If we join in with other churches, what about theological conflicts?"

The short answer: This is respite care, not Sunday school. There won't be a great deal of discussion about theologically divisive topics. There won't be a lot of talk about theology at all.

Chapel services will focus on God and Jesus. You'll talk about God seeing each child, knowing each child's name, and loving each child beyond measure.

That's something you can tell partner churches and tell parents, too.

If parents ask why you're serving them, that's an opportunity to talk about God's love in more depth. This is where denominational nuances may come into play, but if you're partnering with churches that agree with what you consider theological essentials, there will be no major conflicts. The clearest and simplest message is that all people are made in the image of God, so don't let denominational divides get in the way of serving and loving families.

"Aren't there already social service agencies that do this and do it well?"

Maybe, but Jill's House hears from families that finding qualified respite providers is tough. And those who do provide respite will be the first to say they're not fully meeting all the need in your community for respite care. They'll welcome having your church provide care, too.

And the families who benefit from your ministry will certainly welcome it, as well.

And there's this: Most social agencies that provide respite care provide in-home assistance. It's far harder to find organizations that provide respite settings outside the home, which is actually way better according to Jill's House families!

Your program will not only give children who participate a chance to socialize, but you'll give parents a window in which they can catch up on things that need to be done around the home, go to self-care appointments, and to finally take a nap.

Naps are good, too!

"What if we can't continue to fund this ministry once it gets going?"

Denny will help you with that one.

"There's often a question about whether a church has enough money, with an assumption that there are limited resources. Any question that starts there will end up with a decision that whatever is being proposed won't work," he said. "But God doesn't have limited resources. If we're following the will of God, he'll provide the resources. When you're doing God's work, God's way, you won't lack for resources."

Donors respond to unique, transformational ideas like bringing respite care to your community.

So, the question isn't about money, it's about mission. Is God calling your congregation to launch a respite care ministry? If so, move ahead. Denny has provided practical tips for raising funds. You'll get what you really need, but go into the process knowing that fundraising is hard. Be prepared to rely on God's provision and to work hard for the ministry he wants you to provide.

"I'll just admit it: I'm uncomfortable around children with disabilities. I'm not even sure how to talk with them or their families."

Thank you for your honesty. A fear of saying the wrong thing sometimes keeps people from saying anything at all.

And church leaders aren't immune to that concern.

Assure the leaders that you'll provide training for how to handle those potentially embarrassing situations. There's training available in Chapter 21 for your use.

"What if we just don't have the patience to keep working with kids like that?"

First, working with a child with disabilities doesn't require more patience than coming alongside any other child. Anyone who's endured an endless game of "Candy Land" with a young child has explored the outer edges of patience and survived.

What *is* required is empathy and understanding.

Empathy because a child with special needs is living a different life than the one most of your volunteers are living. That doesn't mean it's necessarily a better or worse life; it's just different. Being with that child demands that a volunteer choose to see the world through the eyes of that child.

And serving children requires that a volunteer seek to understand before seeking to be understood.

There may be balance issues as a child moves through a room. Understanding that helps a volunteer be in the right place to offer any assistance that's required.

It's possible a child will be non-verbal or struggle to make herself understood. When a volunteer understands that, the volunteer leans in, stays present in the moment, and considers what the child might want or need.

Forming a friendship with a child who has special needs isn't a matter of patience. It's a matter of *compassion*—and being open to not just serving, but being served in return.

And it is totally worth it in every way imaginable.

When colleagues at work ask what their coworkers did with the weekend, it's always the volunteer who served at Jill's House who has the most rewarding story to share.

And the biggest smile.

"Will a respite ministry really have all that much impact?"

One way to know if a program is making a difference is to stop doing it and to see what happens.

If you disband the choir, will droves of congregants pack up and go? What about if you cancel all children's ministry activities? Youth group? The coffee bar at the back of the sanctuary?

If you're wondering about the impact of providing respite care, get to know Cindy Larson. She had it—and it went away.

"I had three children aged three and under," she says. "I knew what busy felt like."

But then her son, Bridger, came along bringing with him a rare genetic disorder that included global challenges—physical, cognitive, speech, vision, seizures, and g-tube feeding among them.

"All of a sudden my husband and I were living with a new normal," says Cindy. "It's a beautiful normal, but nobody was ever meant to endure this sort of extreme exhaustion long-term."

Cindy discovered Jill's House early on, shortly after the doors opened. She filled out an application and, when Bridger was old enough, Cindy let him try a weekend away.

It was a godsend.

"That first weekend I kept my eye on the phone waiting for a call, but it didn't come. Bridger was doing fine, and we got to enjoy the luxury of sleeping through the night and going out to dinner with the rest of our kids. It was amazing."

Cindy has given up explaining what it's like to raise a child with special needs. "People just don't get it. They don't understand—can't understand," said Cindy. "When you're raising a child like Bridger there's no light at the end of the tunnel. When my other four children run into challenges, I can tell them that things will change with time. But that's not true with Bridger. This is forever. This is from now on. Jill's House becomes a light at the end of our tunnel."

First, there's the anticipation of knowing respite care is coming—and that alone is a lifesaver for Cindy and her husband.

"We can get through a lot of really difficult days knowing that in fourteen days we'll get a weekend of rest," she said.

And then there's this: Because Jill's House swallows Bridger up in love, she can actually rest while her son is away.

"There's no guilt about our taking the other four kids on a fun outing," Cindy said. "We haven't left Bridger behind at home with a nurse. He's having a great time at Jill's House."

Cindy has never had to wonder if her son enjoyed his time away. Though Bridger is largely non-verbal, while driving home after picking him up at the end of the weekend she grew accustomed to hearing Bridger cry out, "More Jill's House! More Jill's House!"

Jill's House is a gift Cindy wishes she could once again give her son, but their family recently moved to Texas where, at least in her area, there's no respite care available.

None. And Cindy's family is feeling the loss.

"I wish a church nearby would do something like what Jill's House has done," she said. "I'm going through respite withdrawal."

If you're sitting in Texas wondering if your church should do respite care, you know how Cindy would vote. If she's anywhere near you and you open your doors to families like hers, she'll find you—and bring with her a family brimming with love and gifts to share with your church.

Respite care has a *huge* impact—in your community, your congregation, and in the lives of families like the Larsons.

CHAPTER 17

RESPITE CARE MINISTRY INTAKE AND RELEASE FORMS

*Y*ou're a visionary with a mission to get a respite care program launched, and the last thing you want to do is wade knee-deep into a swamp of forms, policies, and procedures. You know nothing slows down forward momentum like having to submit every scrap of paper to the Sub-Committee of Form Formation for approval.

But trust us: It pays to get organized up front so you're not playing catch-up later.

Take a deep breath and pause long enough to make decisions about what you need to know and when you need to know it. And how to set parents' expectations about who you are and what you can deliver.

Thinking and talking through these forms, then tweaking them to fit your needs (or starting over from scratch) will help that happen.

Respite Ministry Intake Form

Your intake form is a place to strike a balance.

You don't need to know everything there is to know about a child and the child's medical condition. But you do need to know enough to be sure you're qualified to safely care for the child and to have a sense of the child's preferences.

And something else is happening as well: Your form will either increase or decrease a parent's confidence that your program is a safe place for their child.

When Brenda was caring for Jill as an infant, there were people who now and then offered to stay with Jill while Brenda took a nap or ducked out to make a grocery run.

The problem was that, as kindhearted as those offers were, they were often made by people who didn't have the training to adequately care for Jill.

Sometimes they were made by people who didn't even ask for details concerning Jill's fragile medical condition.

Parents raising special needs children develop quickly a sense about who can—and can't—care well for their children. And one major sign that someone's in the running is if that person asks questions.

The following template for an intake form—which will be part of your application for care—sends a signal loud and clear: We're serious about caring for your child.

Adapt it as you wish or use it as is—you have our permission to copy it for your respite care use.

RESPITE MINISTRY INTAKE FORM

Date: _____

Child's name: _____ Child's age:_____

Child's address: Street: _____

City: _____ State: _____ ZIP: _____

Parent's name: _____

Parent's address: Street:_____

City: _____ State: _____ ZIP: _____

Parent's email address: _____

Parent's cell phone(s):_____Landline:_____Pager:_____

While your child is in our care, what is the best way to reach you?

_____

What is your child's disability diagnosis/diagnoses?

_____

Your child's primary care physicians' name: _____

Your child's primary care physicians' phone number: _____

Current medications: _____

List all known allergies: _____

Emergency contact information:

First contact person:
Name: _____ Phone number: _____

Relationship with child: _____

Second contact person:
Name: _____ Phone number: _____

Relationship with child: _____

How does your child typically respond to being away from you?

_____

How well does your child play with others?

_____

How does your child prefer to communicate?

_____

What assistance might your child require regarding hygienic needs?

_____

What assistance might your child require regarding eating?

_____

What assistance might your child require regarding mobility?

_____

What are common behaviors your child may exhibit?

_____

Please check any of the following that describe your child:
____ Transitions are challenging
____ Changes in routine are challenging
____ Completing tasks is challenging
____ Following directions is challenging
____ Brief attention span
____ Aggressive behavior
____ Shyness
____ Tends to wander away from the group
____ Easily frustrated
____ Tends to be possessive

What's something your child especially enjoys doing?

_____

What delights your child?

_____

What else do you want us to know about your child?

_____

permission to photocopy for local church use granted by the publisher

Respite Care Ministry Release Form

Parents want to know precisely what level of care you're providing and your release form—which they'll sign—is a place to be crystal clear. You don't want to imply that volunteers are certified medical professionals unless they are.

And be careful about stating that a trained nurse will be present during respite sessions unless that will be true every time and, should a nurse be unavailable, you're prepared to cancel the session.

Saying "no" is often the most gracious, loving, and best thing you can say. Raising expectations and then failing to meet them is more disappointing to parents than having had explained at the outset that you're not prepared to meet their need.

Communicate clearly as you present a release form to parents that your goal is to be as informed and up-to-date as possible about the child so you can provide the best possible care during the respite session. If you've done a good job reviewing and vetting intake forms, you'll have only children you think you can manage in each session.

But kids with special needs are just like all kids everywhere, throughout time: They have good days and bad days. You'll want to have a brief conversation as parents bring children into your respite area so you know who's having which sort of day.

And know that no release or permission form is foolproof protection against lawsuits. Medical facilities long ago discovered that negligent care can result in legal consequences, no matter how many forms were signed before treatment.

So, don't be negligent. Train volunteers to focus on the children, put away their phone, and not cluster together to talk as kids play. Model focused care and volunteers will emulate it.

And keep this in mind: Establishing a relationship is not only key to building trust and providing an environment for sharing the Gospel, it's a solid legal strategy, too.

What follows is suggested language used in some local churches, but refer to it to capture the spirit of what you'll need to have signed, not the final version. You'll need to adapt the language to your situation, and clear it with an attorney.

RESPITE MINISTRY RELEASE FORM

I have fully disclosed to [*your church name*] complete and relevant information about my child's special needs, and I accept full responsibility for having done so. I've provided that information on the respite care intake form and updated information while checking my child in for a session of respite care. Those updates are as follows (provide any and all in writing, please):

_____

_____

_____

_____

_____

I understand the respite care ministry is staffed by non-medically certified volunteers whose intent is to provide excellent care for my child.

_____

_____

_____

_____

While my child is enrolled in the respite program, I authorize the volunteers to provide any required special treatments or procedures. I will provide instructions and any needed supplies and equipment for these procedures. By signing this form, I am giving my consent.

In case of an emergency or accident, I understand the local 911 Emergency Medical Services will be called. I authorize EMS to administer any medical treatment, medication, or appliance they deem necessary to treat my child. I also authorize transportation by EMS to the nearest medical facility, as determined by EMS. I accept responsibility for payment of EMS, hospital, and physician charges for services rendered on behalf of my child.

I understand my child's Respite Intake Form, containing medical information I have provided, will be sent with my child to aid in my child's treatment.

I have read this permission/authorization statement and agree to the terms described in it.
I/we agree to hold (First Christian Church) free of any and all legal responsibility in connection with our child's participation in activities with (insert program name).

Signed : _____

Dated : _____

(Parent/Guardian)

permission to photocopy for local church use granted by the publisher

CHAPTER 18

RESPONDING TO BEHAVIORS

𝓝 othing beats actual hands-on training when it comes to learning how to respond to behaviors. That's because this issue is one that most volunteers fear and have zero idea how to navigate.

So do take the time to find training from special needs professionals in the public school or the Health Department.

In the interim, here are some basic principles to put in place as you plan how to organize your respite care ministry. By keeping these in mind, you'll go a long way toward creating an environment that avoids common triggers and prepares your volunteers to respond appropriately when the occasional issue arises.

Banish boredom

Some maladaptive behavior is the result of the frustration that comes with boredom. By shifting activities often—at Jill's House it's roughly every 25 minutes—you keep any one activity from growing stale. By the time a child is becoming bored, you're on to the next activity.

Build in choice

When a craft project or game is suggested at Jill's House, results aren't carved in stone.

Children in the pool may be splashing water, floating, playing with a pool noodle or beach ball—whatever they choose to do.

When children are on the outside play area, there are lots of options for play. Providing choice hands children some measure of control—and any child should be able to choose.

Expect and reinforce capability

Some children with special needs find it difficult to read emotion or know what's appropriate and what isn't.

So tell and show them—explicitly. And then hold kids to that standard. Establishing and reinforcing positive expectations builds self-esteem in children, because you're assuming they can meet the standard.

Establish relationships

We do things for people we know and like because we want to please them. You and the volunteers in your respite care ministry can become those people in the lives of the children you serve.

Get to know and love the kids who come. When you speak to children, make it a policy to use their names. Be approachable and fair. Claim authority in your respite care room but do so kindly—and by earning the respect and trust of the kids.

Get and stay organized

Having a predictable, structured routine helps many children with special needs feel safe. It's okay to be flexible, but have a plan and don't stray too far from it.

You'll reduce the chances of encountering an anxious reaction by having a structure that provides security to children who need it.

Transition carefully

As you move from one area to another or one activity to the next, don't let children become anxious. Instead, tell children what's coming and help them embrace the changes.

Consider having a written schedule on a white board or printed out to show those individuals who are comforted by knowing what's coming and when. Having small, laminated pictures instead of or next to a written schedule can be extremely helpful.

Buddy up

You'll have a volunteer paying close attention to each child, but it's also good for children to have buddies assigned for some activities. Your respite care can launch friendships if you'll make room for relationships to form—and they'll form first around sharing activities.

Create a quiet space option

Some children actively express anxiety or fear when overstimulated. If a child feels as if she's getting to that point, have a way the child can back away from a loud or crowded activity to go read a book, listen to music, or otherwise give herself a break.

Some ministries have a number of laminated "me time" cards that can be claimed at any time so a child can take a break. Need a break? Take a card and go to one of the approved spots in the room. You'll know the child is okay and is self-managing anxiety or if another trigger is in play.

Act

When less than desirable behavior occurs, don't ignore it and hope it goes away. Address it. Come alongside the child and see what you can do to help fix what's wrong. Perhaps turning down the volume in the room will help. Maybe it's adjusting the lighting or helping the child pick another activity. Maybe there's a conflict that can be resolved.

Consult with the intake form and release form to see what they can tell you about a child's preferences and temperament.

But don't pretend nothing is happening and hope it goes away. Doing so can lead to what's now a small challenge growing much, much bigger—quickly.

CHAPTER 19

MEDICAL AND BACKGROUND CHECK INFORMATION

*W*hen a teenager is babysitting, there are just three things that teenager needs to write down: 1) When's bedtime for the child, 2) When the parents will be home, and 3) where the family keeps the Doritos.

You're not just babysitting, and you'll be collecting far more sensitive information from each family you serve.

The Health Insurance Portability and Accountability Act of 1996 (HIPAA) put in place standards for protecting individuals' health information. The Security Rule portion of HIPAA applies to health plans, health care clearinghouses, and any health care provider who transmits health information in electronic form—and that may or may not be you.

But it's expected that you'll protect any health information you collect from families you serve. And the expectation is that you'll meet the standards met elsewhere—all of which are calibrated to HIPAA standards.

In short, you're expected to ensure that information you collect—no matter how you gather it—will remain confidential. And that you'll take appropriate steps to guard against information being disclosed (with or without your permission) to anyone else. Being intentional about taking this step respects the privacy and dignity of those you serve, and it helps to establish the trust you want and need with families.

At minimum, paperwork must be kept in a locked cabinet with limited and controlled access. If you're gathering information online that portion of your website must be adequately firewalled.

Have these ducks lined up before you begin gathering information; you'll be asked by parents who fill out forms about your ability to protect data they're sharing about their children. Jill's House is happy to share their best practices with you.

Background Check Forms

Even volunteers who can't think of anything significant that might show up on a background check sometimes feel intimidated. How about that embarrassing speeding ticket they got 15 years ago? And the two since then?

The answer is that it depends.

It depends on what sort of background check you run. But in almost every case there's going to be something that shows up—and you may need to have a conversation.

If you choose to not accept a volunteer into the ministry, you *definitely* need to have a conversation.

Privately sharing the basis of the denial is your chance to put what may feel like personal rejection into perspective and to help direct the potential volunteer toward another area of service within the church or community.

And it's equally important that you be careful about handling each and every background check you collect. It's sensitive information, and you need a process in place to keep it secure and confidential.

If you have hard copies, lock them in a secure file and office. If there's an electronic version, keep it on a computer that's password protected and has limited and controlled access.

How long an organization is required to keep background checks varies from state to state, but because sexual abuse claims may be filed decades after a volunteer serves in an organization, the prevailing wisdom holds that you keep records forever.

If arranging perpetual for anything sounds daunting—and it is—inquire if your background check provider can arrange for the storage of background checks.

By the way, don't forget to update your background checks frequently. Check with your background check provider and local organizations to determine frequency. It is also a good idea to check with a local attorney to look over your process.

CHAPTER 20

VOLUNTEER FORMS AND INFORMATION

*W*ithout volunteers, you won't have a ministry.

And without ministering to those volunteers by providing what they need to serve well and with confidence, you won't have volunteers.

The forms you'll find here will pop you over into the express lane as you prepare a volunteer-friendly environment, one that will help you hang onto one of the most precious assets your ministry will ever have: your volunteers.

Feel free to photocopy the forms in this chapter for your local church use or, even better, adapt them to fit your unique situation.

Volunteer Expectation Checklist

If you've ever agreed to help someone, only to find out the actual project is far, far larger than what you were told, you know why experienced volunteers are skeptical of signing on without full disclosure.

They want to know what you're asking them to do, how long you expect them to serve, and where there's an exit ramp in case they're not a fit with the role.

Your Volunteer Expectation Checklist is how all that gets said. Because it's not just what you're expecting from volunteers, but what *they* can expect from *you*.

You'll have to craft your own checklist, but we have some suggestions about what should be included:

• **A Clear Mission Statement**

The world is knee-deep in half-finished mission statements or statements that were lifted almost verbatim from other organizations.

Maybe that's because it's easy to over think a mission statement, to spend so long wordsmithing to get committee approval that it's easier to walk away and live without a statement. Or worse, to end up with one that's elegant, uplifting, and essentially useless.

So, write yours the easy way.

Answer these three questions, as briefly as you can, in this order:

What's our vision? (Example: We want to provide respite care to as many families raising children with disabilities as possible.)

What are three core values that will inform our decisions and behavior? (Example: We want to proclaim the Gospel, serve parents, and love children.)

What are our goals and objectives? (Example: We want to convert three rooms in our church into accessible space, recruit and train an adequate number of volunteers, and get this ministry up and running by September 1.)

Now mash those up, print what you have in a nice font, and there's your mission statement. Any potential volunteer knows exactly where he or she is being asked to go, what values will drive decisions, and what has to happen to make it all work.

Now it's easy to say "yes" or "no" to a request about helping because the ask is in focus.

To give even greater clarity to what you're intending to accomplish and what you value as you go about it, consider creating a visual representation of your mission. Reproduced for you here is how Jill's House sums up what it's about in a simple, read-it-in-30 seconds visual summary. It's reproduced with Jill's House permission.

THE JILL'S HOUSE PYRAMID

Everything we do points families to
our Lord and Savior, Jesus Christ

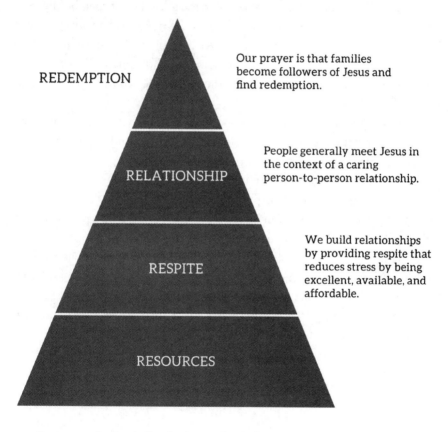

REDEMPTION — Our prayer is that families become followers of Jesus and find redemption.

RELATIONSHIP — People generally meet Jesus in the context of a caring person-to-person relationship.

RESPITE — We build relationships by providing respite that reduces stress by being excellent, available, and affordable.

RESOURCES

Resources–funds, staff, volunteers, physical space, etc.
–make respite available.

But just as important as a mission statement is a statement of faith.

• A Statement of Faith

Your organization cares about accomplishing tasks. You're a faith-based ministry, and that gives you a unique take on respite care.

Like your friends at Jill's House, you see respite care as more than *just* respite care. It's ministry—and a way to exercise and share your faith.

"At Jill's House we're called to proclaim the Gospel boldly and clearly to the families we serve," said Joel. "We're called to love without distinction, whether families we serve ever come to faith and whatever their faith backgrounds. We don't view the families who come to Jill's House as just consumers of respite care. We see them as whole people to be loved and served."

To sustain that sort of servanthood takes more than sheer determination. It requires having a team that's fueled by God's love and motivated by an understanding that God's in this.

It requires a statement of faith.

This sample statement is provided as an example to emulate, not just to appropriate. It's clear, concise, and directly connects the ministry with biblical beliefs that support the ministry.

The process of grappling with creating a faith statement is of great value. It clarifies *why* you're launching a respite care ministry. It identifies what beliefs undergird every decision you'll make moving forward. And it's something to show potential volunteers to let them know the foundation of your ministry.

[FIRST CHRISTIAN CHURCH'S]
RESPITE CARE MINISTRY STATEMENT OF FAITH

*W*e believe all people are created in God's image. There's no minimum IQ required or set of abilities needed. Connection to God is a free gift, freely given by God.

*W*e believe we're called to love our neighbors and do so in practical ways that reflect the love God has so generously showered on us.

*W*e believe we're to love without reservation—to love those who know God and those who don't. To love those who believe and those who don't yet believe.

*W*e believe we're called to clearly proclaim Jesus, with our actions and also our words. We're not ashamed of or uncertain about the Gospel, knowing it's the power of God at work, saving all who trust Jesus.

*W*e believe we are called to care. Called to pray. Called to do. And we believe God has prompted us to embrace respite care as one way he's loving his people in our community through us.

- **Clear Expectations of Volunteers**
  Here's where you set the bar—and set it high.
  Again, you'll want to fill your Volunteer Expectation Checklist with your own expectations, but here are some that you might consider including and some possible language to get you started.
  Required Training: Before volunteers serve, they will complete a required one-hour training session that will familiarize them with the ministry, cover essential information, and provide a grounding in essential skills. A further training session specific to the volunteer's role will follow, as well as one respite session spent shadowing an established volunteer.

Frequency and Length of Service: Volunteers are expected to serve once per month for a period of one year.

Qualifications: Prospective volunteers do not need any previous experience working with children who have disabilities, but are expected to pass a background check.

Quarterly Staff Meetings: Volunteers will meet as a group twice per year to receive information and ongoing training.

Periodic Evaluations: Volunteers will meet with the Respite Ministry Coordinator several times per year to discuss performance and to discuss any issues needing resolution.

As you complete your checklist of expectations, be as specific as possible.

• **Clear Expectations Volunteers Can Have of You**

If you're planning to hang on to volunteers, let them know from the outset what they can expect from you.

Among other expectations, list these:

Adequate and Ongoing Training: You won't toss volunteers into a room and expect them to figure things out.

Flexibility in Scheduling: They can expect to serve one shift each month, and more if they desire, but you'll do your best to provide flexible scheduling.

Ongoing Access: Each volunteer will have the cell phone number of the Respite Care Coordinator so if issues arise, they can be dealt with directly and swiftly.

Gratitude: You appreciate the volunteers and so do the children and families they'll serve.

Sample Volunteer Expectation Sheet

The following is a sample Volunteer Expectation Sheet. Its purpose is to sum up what you're expecting so potential volunteers can see at a glance what they're being asked to do. It's what you'll hand people if you have an information table in the back of the lobby after worship services some weekend.

This isn't a formal job description. Nor does it answer every question that might arise—and that's by intent.

This form will weed out potential volunteers who aren't willing to see respite care as more than babysitting—those are people you don't really want on the team. This form will also prompt questions from people who are truly interested, and you'll have a chance to talk with them one-on-one so you can get a sense of how they'll fit into your team.

Have the attorney for your church review these sample forms—and all forms—you plan on distributing.

[FIRST CHRISTIAN CHURCH]
RESPITE CARE VOLUNTEER EXPECTATION LIST
(CAREGIVER)

Wondering exactly what's expected of you if you serve as a Respite Caregiver? Here's a brief description of what's involved:

- My first responsibility will be to treat, with loving respect, the children with special needs who take part in our program. I will extend the same respect and concern to the families of children we serve.

- I understand that I will be given information about the children I will serve. This information will include medical information and information about behavioral characteristics and food. I agree to read this information prior to providing care and to treat the information as confidential. I will share information only with other members of the [First Christian] Respite Care Team as needed to provide adequate care.

- I will engage children in play and conversation.

- I will assist in the restroom in accordance with the policies and procedures of the Respite Care Ministry.

- I will be ready and at my post a minimum of 20 minutes before the start of the respite care session and stay until the last child is picked up, unless otherwise directed by the team leader.

- I will pass the mandatory respite care training provided by First Christian Church and will attend quarterly team meetings.

- I will also be required to take and pass a background screening, whose results will be kept confidential but be considered as I seek this volunteer position.

- I will report any difficulties I experience in my role as a Respite Caregiver to the team leader promptly.

- I am aware that serving in this ministry may put my personal safety at risk, and I will be required to sign a form releasing [First Christian Church] from any liability in regard to my personal safety.

- Assuming this role is one in which I'm successful, I am committing to serve once a month for one year. I may be asked to serve more often as the ministry grows and will consider doing so—but I'm under no obligation to agree to additional shifts.

RESPITE CARE VOLUNTEER JOB DESCRIPTION AND RELEASE FORM (CAREGIVER)

The mission of the [First Christian] Respite Care Ministry is to provide respite care to as many families raising children with disabilities as possible. As we do so, we'll proclaim the Gospel, serve parents, and love children—unconditionally.

As a Caregiver I will…
- Embrace the mission of the Respite Care Ministry and promote it through my words and actions.

- Keep confidential medical and personal history information about children I serve and their families, strictly adhering to the ministry team's policies and procedures.

- I will engage children in a variety of activities, including but not limited to: crafts, games, creative movement, and singing.

- In accordance with the policies and procedures of the Respite Care Ministry, I will assist children with toileting needs.

- I will be ready and at my post a minimum of 20 minutes before the start of the respite care session and stay until the last child is picked up, unless otherwise directed by the team leader.

- I will complete initial training and also attend quarterly team meetings.

- I will report any difficulties I experience in my role as a Respite Caregiver to the team leader promptly.

- I will commit, as best as I am able, to serve for one year in this ministry.

I have read the above description of my ministry role and agree to abide by all rules and directives of [First Christian Church] in relation to my volunteer role with the Respite Care Ministry.

I also acknowledge that serving in this ministry may put my personal safety at risk, so I hereby release [First Christian Church] from any liability in regard to my personal safety.

Signed this _____ day of _____, 2_____.

Name: _____
(Please Print)

_____

Volunteer Signature

Address: _____

City, State, Zip _____

Phone Number: _____ Email: _____

*We advise that you consult with an attorney regarding liability concerns, as simply having a liability release on file, while a good practice, does not in itself fully protect a ministry from a potential lawsuit.

[FIRST CHRISTIAN CHURCH]
RESPITE MINISTRY VOLUNTEER EVALUATION FORM

Name: _____ Date: _____

Team Leader: _____

Rating scale: 1: could use improvement
                 2: fine
                 3: excellent
                 4. world class

_____ Demonstrates an understanding of the purpose and goals of the Respite Care Ministry

_____ Engages with children

_____ Engages with parents

_____ Keeps confidential information confidential

_____ Enthusiastically enters into activities with children

_____ Adheres to ministry policies and protocols

_____ Is reliably on time and stays as long as is needed

_____ Attends and participates in team meetings

_____ Communicates directly

_____ Exhibits poise when difficult situations arise.

_____ Demonstrates compassion and understanding with children parents, and team members

_____ Is willing to go the extra mile in fulfilling duties.

_____ Asks questions when in doubt

Comments: _____

_____

_____

_____

Signature of Ministry Team Leader : _____ Date: _____

Signature of Volunteer: _____ Date: _____

[FIRST CHRISTIAN CHURCH]
RESPITE MINISTRY EVALUATION FORM—TO BE
COMPLETED BY VOLUNTEERS

Team Leader evaluated: _____ Date: _____

Volunteer name: _____

Rating scale: 1: could use improvement
                2: fine
                3: excellent
                4. world class

_____ Thoroughly explained the purpose and goals of the Respite Care Ministry

_____ Provided a job description that clearly defined by role

_____ Engages with me to make sure I'm enjoying serving

_____ Is available and approachable when I have questions

_____ Enthusiastically enters into activities with children

_____ Adheres to ministry policies and protocols

_____ Is reliably on time and stays as long as is needed

_____ Communicates directly

_____ Exhibits poise when difficult situations arise.

_____ Demonstrates compassion and understanding with children parents, and team members

_____ Is willing to go the extra mile in fulfilling duties.

_____ Authentically cares about me as a person

Comments: _____

_____

_____

_____

Please share your responses to these questions:

What additional training would you like to see offered?

_____

_____

What additional resources would make you more effective in your role?

_____

_____

What could the Team Leader or Ministry in general do to make your experience serving better?

_____

_____

Signature of Volunteer: _____ Date: _____

Signature of Team Leader: _____ Date: _____

Recognizing Volunteers

Let's just decide at the outset that one more coffee cup with "#1 Volunteer!" printed on it isn't the answer. Neither is a one-size-fits-all plaque.

The most meaningful recognition is personal—not something that's the same for everyone. That puts some pressure on the Respite Care Team Leader, but here's an easy solution: Send a thank-you card timed to arrive at exactly six months after the volunteer began serving. Thank the volunteer for six months of faithful service. Mention one way the volunteer shines. That you remembered when the volunteer began serving will warm that volunteer's heart.

And six months is the perfect timing for recognition in a one-year commitment. You'll reset the clock for your volunteer and greatly enhance the chance of that person signing up again.

The more personal you can make the recognition, the more powerful it will be. If you know the person collects inkwells or elephant figurines, let that and a heartfelt "thanks" carry the message for you.

And if your team is close and clicking along, a shared pizza meal allows you to encourage laughter, peer affirmation, and storytelling. Make an evening of it!

CHAPTER 21

ETIQUETTE 101 FOR COMMUNICATING WITH PEOPLE WITH SPECIAL NEEDS

*J*n the course of your respite program, you'll be in relationship with a wide range of children and their families. Some children are verbal, some aren't. Some can easily understand you, some can't.

But all must be treated with caring respect.

Unless your volunteers have previous experience relating to a wide range of people with special needs, they may be uncertain just how it looks to communicate that respect as they interact with children and parents.

Share these pointers to help your volunteers get past feeling awkward, to a place where they're comfortable being engaged. But before you provide training, check in with a few families you'll be serving to see if there's anything they'd add to the list.

1. Speak directly to the child, not the child's parent.

Until you know otherwise, assume a child can hear and understand you and answer for him or her self. If and when it becomes clear that you'll need to communicate through the parents, then do so.

And please: Don't increase your volume while speaking to a child with special needs unless that child has a hearing loss.

2. Use "person-first" language.

People with disabilities are more than their disabilities. Were you to be diagnosed with skin cancer, it's doubtful you'd want to be introduced as, "This is my cancerous friend, Daniel."

Less offensive, and if there's any need to refer to your cancer at all, would be to say, "This is my friend Daniel, who has cancer."

People with special needs of any kind generally don't want to be described primarily as their disability.

Nor is it helpful to refer to people with special needs as "victims." Language that promotes pity or implies that someone with special needs is somehow "less" or "other" builds walls—not bridges.

Few families raising children with special needs are as prickly as people fear. A genuinely kind smile and caring heart can more than compensate for a grammar gaffe—but it's better when those families are greeted with both kindness and a sensitivity to labels and stereotypes.

For the purposes of training your team, here are a few person-first phrases to become familiar with:

Instead of saying...	Say this instead...
The disabled or handicapped	People with disabilities
He's autistic...	He is on the autism spectrum
Healthy kids...	Typical kids...
He's a cripple...	He has a physical disability
Wheel-chair bound...	A person who uses a wheelchair
He's special ed...	He receives special education services
He's an epileptic...	He's a person with epilepsy
He's mentally ill...	He has a mental health condition
He's brain-damaged...	He has a brain injury
Handicapped parking...	Accessible parking
He's retarded...	He has a diagnosis of cognitive impairment
CP sufferer...	A person with cerebral palsy

3. Ask before you help

If you've done a good job interviewing using an intake form, you'll have a fairly good idea what a child can and can't do alone.

Still, check before leaping in to assist with tasks. A child may have worked hard to be able to do tasks on his or her own, so don't needlessly remove the dignity that comes with expressing some independence and self-reliance.

4. Be careful about physical contact

It can be a trigger for some children with specific disabilities, and it can be offensive to anyone. Respect the personal space of someone with the disabilities as much as you respect the physical space of typical people.

Which isn't to say that some kids aren't huggers—they are. But they're also vulnerable, so don't assume that a hug will necessarily be welcomed.

5. Avoid making assumptions

When presenting an activity or game to a child with special needs, leave it up to that child whether he will or won't be able to participate. Encourage kids to give new activities a try, but don't insist.

6. Accommodate—don't coddle

It can be easy to patronize a person with special needs. The best information you have is that if a child can handle a specific task at home, that child can handle it while in respite care setting. You may need to provide guidance, but don't rush to do for children what they can do for themselves.

7. Be patient while communicating

Some people with disabilities may slur speech or not speak at all. You can imagine how frustrating it is for a child to want or need something, but be unable to tell you what it is. If you can't understand what the child is saying, it's ok to ask the child to repeat himself.

Repeat what you do understand; it will help the child know what you still need to know. Don't rush to finish the other person's sentences or pretend you understand more than you actually understand.

If you simply can't make out what's being said, see if the context and timing of the request might give you a clue and check to see if your understanding is accurate.

8. Adjust your posture to be eye-to-eye while communicating

When someone is looming over you, speaking down, it's easy to feel inferior. Don't do that. Instead, lean down or sit down to be on the same level as the child.

9. Don't ignore people with special needs

Afraid they'll say or do the wrong thing, many people opt to just look past people with disabilities...and that's hurtful.

When interacting with children, some who to the untrained eye may seem lost in their own worlds, it's easy to think they won't notice being slighted. But they might. And their parents most certainly will take note.

So, don't pretend you don't see people with disabilities. They have dignity, too. Treat them with regard and respect.

10. Be open to learning a new language

All communication involves choosing to stay engaged, even when there are hurdles to clear on both sides of the conversation. That's true whether the conversation is with a typical person or a non-verbal child.

So commit to getting over the hurdles. A smile, a kind nod, a gentle, reassuring hand on a shoulder—all speak volumes about acceptance and love.

Be open to learning what will connect with a child and don't be discouraged if it takes time to discover what that is.

The joy of connecting makes it all worthwhile.

CHAPTER 22

CAMPS AND RETREATS

*A*lthough Jill's House is blessed to have a tremendous building in which to offer respite programs, they know replicating something of their size is a financial stretch. So in order to expand their respite reach, Jill's House also utilizes a "camp" model.

This approach enables Jill's House to offer respite programming in different locations utilizing existing facilities. By renting space at a camp, Jill's House—and you—can offer all the pluses of overnight respite without the cost of construction, maintenance, and overhead.

While it's true the disabilities experienced by children with special needs vary widely, the children themselves have a great deal in common.

They all want to be loved and to give love in return.

They all want to feel safe and be safe.

And because they're all kids, they want to have fun.

Taking your respite care ministry to a local camp lets you give kids and their families all of that—if you plan ahead.

Here's some help thinking through that planning.

Picking a camp location

The next decision you'll make once you've decided to offer a camp experience is where to go.

There are camping facilities specially designed for children with disabilities, but they may be far from you and already have in place their own prescribed staff and programming.

Programming that may lack a faith component.

Which means you may find yourself drawing a circle around your church building and deciding that whatever camp lies within that circle—a 45-minute drive, perhaps—is a possibility. Anything further away, however nice, is simply too far away for parents to drive to take and pick up their children. Or too far away for your comfort level.

However wide your circle, once you narrow down your camp options to a few contenders, call the camp manager to ask a few questions.

Better yet, make an appointment and visit the camp for a manager-led tour of the facilities. Take photos as you go so you can show parents where their children will be and what activities they'll be enjoying while at camp.

And don't go alone. Round up a few members of your team for a group field trip. Your team members will see the camp through different eyes and may raise questions you don't think to ask.

If there's still some room in the van, bring along a family you serve—including their child with special needs.

See how enthused they are with the facility. Watch as their child navigates the spaces. The feedback you receive will go a long way toward deciding where to hold your camp. And if one of the families you serve enthusiastically endorses the location, half of your marketing has just been done for you.

A few questions to toss at the camp manager at your meeting are these:

"Just how accessible is your camp?"

Few camps were initially built with access for children with special needs in mind, especially camps built before the 1960's. While accommodations may have been made through the years, check to see how accessible the grounds are for wheelchairs and how easy it is for children to use restrooms and beds.

The traditional camp cabin packed with bunk beds may work well for some kids, but it's probably not suitable for your experience.

Take note of the pick-up and drop-off area as well. Is it wheelchair accessible? Well-situated and built so it's easy to get from the parking lot onto a sidewalk or path?

Are ramps and rails in evidence—and where you'd expect them to be?

Check which of the activities listed on the camp's website can be enjoyed by the children you serve, too. Most will be fine—and many of the others can be adapted to work for a wide range of children.

Plan how to make those adaptations *now*—before you get to camp and realize that only children who can climb up and over rails can get aboard the wagon to enjoy a hayride. Keep in mind that Jill's House has discovered that wheelchair accessibility doesn't have to be a deal breaker. There are ways to adapt. If a camp is fully accessible, great! If not, think outside the box for potential solutions.

"How many sessions have you hosted for children with special needs?"

If you're just renting the space and will provide all the staff and programming, it's fine of the answer is "none." You won't be counting on the camp for anything but providing running water and electricity.

But if the camp expects its staff to interact with campers in any capacity, you might want to reconsider your choice of camps.

First, you'll need to vet the camp staff and have them up to speed with a current background check. You'll have to check individual certifications for working with your campers with special needs.

It may be that the camp's internal hiring process includes background checks, and you can quickly provide some training to camp staff who'll interact with your children. A few quick questions will let you know.

You'll need to brief camp staff on your ministry's policies and procedures and ensure they'll comply. Plus, there's setting firm expectations about what the camp staff will do and what you'll do and informing the camp team about the spiritual portion of your programming.

At one camp Jill's House uses, camp personnel help with activities from canoeing, the zip line, and obstacle course.

The staff at this camp—and likely many camps—is open to learning how to serve children with special needs. As you develop a relationship with this camp, see if this is a possibility. It's one more way to spread disability awareness and inclusion.

Though it's also still a good idea to ask about other groups serving children with special needs that have made use of the camp. Get their names and contact them to see what their experiences were like.

"What are your concerns about working with us?"

There may be none—and that would be wonderful.

But if the camp has never or seldom served children with special needs in the past, your meeting with the camp manager is the time to discuss any concerns the manager might have.

One concern you can count on being raised has to do with liability. There's not a camp manager on the planet who doesn't think daily about liability.

Jill's House gets ahead of that question by addressing liability at the outset.

"We have parents sign a liability waiver for the camp and for us," said Dana. "And because it's Jill's House running the program, we have coverage under our insurance policy. We also ask the camps to list us as an 'additional insured' under their existing insurance policy—no camp has ever objected."

But liability concerns aren't primarily about lawsuits. They're also about the safety of the children attending camp and the trust you're building with families.

"Some kids on the autism spectrum are prone to walking away from a group or not staying focused on the activity at hand," said Dana. "So, if we've got someone who likes to wander—someone with a history of suddenly taking off—we don't bring them to camp. If there's a child in a wheelchair and the camp doesn't have paved paths, those children don't go to camp. If a child is medically fragile, we won't bring that child along, either."

The sad reality is that some children who can be served well at Jill's House can't be served well at camp. But those children who are eligible can try things they won't be able to try at Jill's House.

"Some of our camp facilities have high rope courses and zip lines; that's certainly not something we have at Jill's House," said Dana. "Camp offers a different flavor of experience than children get in our building."

Liability also extends to your volunteers. If in your respite care ministry, you have a policy of never having a child be alone with a volunteer, maintain that standard while you're at camp. A camp is a change of venue, not a shift in policies or procedures.

And to be clear: a Jill's House camp is for children, not their entire families.

Parents may choose to transport their children to the camp facility, but they then quickly back up the van and head home for a time of respite while Jill's House staff and volunteers spend time with their children.

Jill's House Retreats are another matter.

"Our retreats are an extension of the Jill's House Family Support ministry team, the 'tip of the spear' in our evangelistic outreach to families," said Dana.

The Family Support team ministers in a holistic way, and four yearly retreats are where attendees encounter the message of the Gospel and the hope it brings.

"One retreat is for the entire family," said Dana. "We provide lodging and food for an entire weekend in a rural retreat setting. We also provide child care and programming for both the children with special needs and for the neurotypical children."

The family retreat is structured to include free time as well as structured activities—including speaker sessions during which parents hear from someone experienced with the challenges and joy disability can bring to families. Speakers share their own stories and speak frankly about how their Christian faith has equipped them through their journey.

"We discuss issues like anxiety, fear, anger, disappointment, and exhaustion, allowing our faith in a loving heavenly Father to inform the discussion," said Dana.

A quick caution: be careful about selecting your speakers. It matters that a speaker understands the world of a family with children with special needs. The speaker needs to communicate warmth and understanding while connecting the peace found in Jesus with the peace needed in any busy life.

Jill's House also holds a marriage retreat each year. During this retreat, parents leave children at home so they can concentrate on each other and dedicate time to their relationship.

"During our Single Moms' Retreat we pamper moms with childcare, healthy food, an afternoon tea, and a free carwash. This weekend creates a safe place for these mothers raising children on their own to process their lives, sharing with other women who understand exactly what they're going through," said Dana. "Our retreat speaker talks about God's provision and grace through times of loneliness, uncertainty, and fear of the future."

And then there's a retreat just for fathers.

Because there's a stereotype that men aren't about to open up about challenges in their lives, and that if you take guys out to the woods for a few days there had better be hunting, fishing, hatchet throwing, and beer, we'll pause to take a closer look at this fourth Jill's House retreat.

We'll begin by asking: What do a dozen dads talk about when they're together in the woods?

"Pretty much everything," said Mike Stralow, who led the most recent Jill's House Dads' Retreat.

"We went into this 24-hour overnight retreat without a firm agenda—that was a strategic decision," said Mike. "Dads come into this retreat stressed and packing in a lot of activities doesn't help with that."

Mike describes one dad sharing that his life had fallen into a cycle: His days at work were demanding and stressful, with more to do than he could accomplish in eight hours.

But when he got home—following a stressful commute—he came through the door to find his wife had experienced an even *more* stressful day caring for their son, whose characteristics came with a significant dose of aggressive behavior.

So, to give his wife a break, this father put aside his laptop and spent the evening caring for their son. Then it was up before dawn, to hurry through the work he hadn't finished the day before, and another commute into the office. Another stressful day, another commute home—you get the picture.

The last thing this dad needed was to be handed a sheet of activities planned out to the minute.

What he *did* need was 24 hours of time to just...be. Twenty-four hours of time for himself.

And he needed the chance to see he wasn't alone—to be with other dads whose lives included children with disabilities.

Mike shares a principle that guides all programming provided at Jill's House: "The recipe is simple, but the impact is profound."

That is, Jill's House is in the business of providing rest, not entertainment. If Jill's House were a theme park attraction, it would be a quiet river ride, not a roller coaster.

"We offer parents a timeout from the rest of their lives," said Mike. "We provide a time and opportunity for rest and relationship."

With those goals in mind, here are Mike's tips for launching a Dads' Retreat:

• **Right size your expectations.** "When you first get started, keep your expectations realistic," he said. "We had 15 dads come, but if you get four or five, that's fine. These are busy people, and some of the dads who need this the most may not be able to get away to come."

Stick with it, Mike suggests. Word of mouth is important, so deliver a great experience and the dads who participate will invite those who need to come.

• **Don't over-program.** "Have a few talking points and some discussion points, but don't overdo it. These dads are often so starved for conversation that they'll take it from there," said Mike.

One way to ensure a deeper conversation is to encourage dads to talk about their kids. "That quickly moves things below the surface," said Mike.

• **See your retreat as a launch pad.** "Once these guys got talking, they discovered they had a lot in common," Mike said. "A couple of them even realized they work in the same building downtown. Different agencies, so they never ran into one another, but the same building." These men exchanged contact information and made plans to get together for lunch to keep the conversations going.

"We had some dads whose kids were older emerge as mentors to younger dads," said Mike. Those relationships wouldn't have happened without the retreat—and will bear fruit long after the retreat.

And if you're wondering whether organizing retreats is worth the effort, be sure to ask Dr. Subarna Dharia before you make a final decision.

Subarna, a pediatrician in northern Virginia, heard about Jill's House while construction was still underway. "I'm not a Christian, but I knew McLean Bible Church was providing a few hours of respite care and I felt comfortable giving it a try."

When Jill's House first opened its doors, Subarna's son Rohan was too young to stay there. But as Rohan grew older, he became a repeat guest.

Happy with that experience, Subarna was quick to say "yes" when asked if she and her family of five would like to be part of the first Family Retreat.

"It was a turning point," said Subarna. "That's when I first fully realized how the Jill's House Staff really felt about Rohan and other people with disabilities. I saw pure love for Rohan, something I couldn't expect from anyone other than our family. It was amazing—I could see love in their faces and all of their actions."

Later, asked if she'd go to another retreat to support families who were attending for the first time, this busy physician, wife, and mother made it happen.

"What the retreat does for families is remarkable," said Subarna. "It's rare for families like ours to all have fun while on vacation, to have something for all of us to enjoy. But at the retreat, that happened. And there was both physical *and* emotional support.

There were times for moms to get together to talk while staff from Jill's House cared for the children. Dads had the same opportunity to connect.

"My husband is still in touch with one man he met there," Subarna said. "Rohan's two brothers had so much fun with the siblings of the children with special needs—and Rohan had fun, too. I came home wanting every family in the Jill's House community to experience a retreat. Every family."

You may or may not choose to add camps or retreats to your respite care ministry, but if you do, ponder these issues:

How well can we staff the event?

Being in a new environment can trigger anxiety in some children. Having extra volunteers on hand at a camp setting so you can lower your volunteer-to-child ratio is a good idea.

If you're staffing a retreat, you'll have the benefit of having parents with their children a good deal of the time, so staffing may not be an issue. But be aware that lining up volunteers for an entire weekend for a retreat, or perhaps even longer at a camp, can be challenging.

How will we address meal preparation?

A camp kitchen may not be set up to easily avoid cross-contamination of foods. If food intolerances and allergies are a factor for the children you serve, spend time in the kitchen planning how you'll handle meal preparation during your camp tour.

Planning a menu can also be problematic. Children with disabilities may be on special diets—gluten free, high or low calorie, high or low fat, or ketogenic, among others.

Carry your concerns out into the dining area as well. Is there adequate room between tables for children using wheelchairs? Are the tables and food-serving counters low enough to accommodate all your children?

You may find you won't be able to prepare one-size-fits-all dinners; you'll have a half-dozen individual meals to prepare and have ready to serve at one time.

Feeding individual campers the right food isn't an insurmountable challenge, but it does require pre-planning and preparation.

What medical facilities are in the area should an emergency arise?

Many camps are rural, so getting to an emergency room may take longer than you find comfortable. Ambulance and 9-1-1 response times may be slower than in a more populated area, too.

Those two realities speak to having a nurse with you at your retreat and information already gathered about who to call should the need arise. Also, check with the camp to see if they have a registered nurse on staff.

What sort of programming will you provide?

Take full advantage of the activities available at the camp facility itself.

If there's a lake, and weather and staffing permits, let kids enjoy the water. If there's a rope course or zip line and they can be used safely, arrange to use them.

The goal isn't to do what you'd usually do in your respite program, just with a better view out the window. You're giving kids experiences they can't get at home, so if you're out in the woods, go for a hike, find wildflowers, or sit outside around a campfire toasting s'mores and telling tall tales.

Do the things that have made summer camp fun for decades—with an emphasis on having fun, building friendships, and encouraging participation.

Dive into your program planning with a focus on abilities rather than what a child can't do. Do all you can to let children participate as fully as possible—it builds confidence and makes memories.

But be mindful that some medical conditions make excessive heat or strenuous activity difficult. As always, have options available if some children grow tired or choose to quit participating mid-activity. And if a child simply can't participate in an activity, ask the child what portion of the activity the child can do—and do it alongside the child with enthusiasm.

If you're looking for games and activities that can be adapted for campers of all abilities that you may need to pull out if an afternoon thunderstorm cancels the tadpole-catching expedition, here's a quick list:

• **No-Lane Bowling**: Form two teams and use painter's tape to create a dividing line down the center of the room. Place teams on both sides of the line and, using empty soda bottles, set up "pins' on both sides of the lines. The goal is to roll or toss soft balls and knock down the other team's pins. If a pin goes down on one side, the other team can return one of its pins to play. Play until all the pins on one side are knocked over or time runs out. There's no crossing the line, so children with mobility challenges can still easily play.

• **Dress-Up Relay**: Form teams and place easily-accessible boxes of coats, hats, boas, and other clothing items at the other side of the room. The goal is for each team to take turns getting team members to the boxes where they'll put on a clothing item, and then go back to the starting point so the next team member can do the same. A variation: Place a volunteer next to each box and all team members in the relay will add a layer of clothing to their volunteer.

• **Dance Party**: Fire up the music, hand out streamers on sticks, and let children groove and move. Volunteers, too! Save money on streamers by making your own with dowels and colorful crepe paper or nylon fabric. Mix it up by having children use their streamers to keep the beat, write their names in the air, or create swirls in the sky.

• **Sculpture Play**: Small tubs of modeling putty or Play-doh can turn into a mountain of fun when children are challenged to sculpt make-believe pets, favorite superheroes, or to create shapes that reflect their feelings. Letting the dough dry (or helping that along by placing it in a low-temp oven for a few hours) gives children a memento of the retreat to take home.

• **Shrinking Planet**: Using a rope, create a circle on the floor. Have all the kids and volunteers get inside it and then, in incremental steps, shrink the circle to see how far you can go before the people inside just can't fit any longer.

• **Trash Can Basketball**: Use foam balls and a clean trash can—placed on the floor—and either challenge children to shoot three-pointers or take turns showing style while dunking a ball. A variation: Use two cans and play an actual game using passing to move the ball rather than dribbling.

• **Move Along**: Show a fitness video and challenge kids and volunteers to do their best to move along with the exercises being demonstrated.

• **Parachute Fun**: The beauty of bringing a parachute on your retreat is that it's easy to pack, and there are a wide range of games that can be played and adapted for all abilities and age levels.

All games start by laying the parachute flat on the floor and having children and volunteers surround it and hold the edges. An alternative approach is to have children all be seated in chairs (or wheelchairs) so there's no need to lay the parachute flat. Then use these variations or add your own to create a game:

> **Launch Pad**: Place soft objects on the parachute and, as children move their arms up and down, see if you can launch the object like a rocket into space.

> **Colorful Cloud**: Help children coordinate their up-and-down arm movements so the parachute billows up and gently settles down.

> **Balance Ball**: Place an inflated beach ball on the parachute and see if children can keep the ball from falling off as they raise and lower

their arms while holding the parachute. Alternately, see if they can get the ball to fall off—anywhere but in front of themselves.

Hide-Out: In this variation, the children gather in the center of the floor and volunteers billow the parachute up to let it gently settle down over the children.

Ripple Sky: Holding the parachute at shoulder height, the volunteers shake the parachute so it forms a rippling expanse over their heads.

Chase the Mouse: A parachute classic, but one that may be difficult to have be fully inclusive, involves children sitting on the floor and holding the chute at lap height. One child hides under the chute and another gets on it. The goal is for the "cat"—the child on top of the chute—to tag the "mouse," who's hiding beneath it. Rounds of 45 seconds give everyone who wants to be either a cat or mouse to have a turn.

With all games, keep in mind that inclusion suggests that keeping players in the game is better than eliminating players who then have to sit on the sidelines. Most games can be modified so there's little or no elimination of players.

Also, encourage participation in games, but don't insist on it. Some children will be ready to play a given game and others won't. Have alternative activities a child can play with or without an adult volunteer.

Some of those ready-at-an-instant alternatives are having a book to read, a game to play on a volunteer's tablet, or a simple jigsaw puzzle that's set up on a nearby table.

Keeping your retreat simple means you're also allowing time for rest and relaxation.

CHAPTER 23

SEMINAR TOPICS

*P*roviding seminars is another ministry initiative of the Family Support Team.

"The level of trust we build through our respite programming creates a willingness in our parents to turn to us for information and advice outside of respite services," said Dana. "We bring in speakers to address topics of interest and provide childcare so parents can listen to what's presented without interruption."

The following are ten topics that parents of children with special needs report are both relevant and helpful:

Financial planning

How do I arrange my finances to best provide care for my child throughout their life and after mine? What should I be keeping in mind?

Coping with my own emotions

This isn't what I expected parenting to be like. How do I make peace with grief and a reality I didn't choose?

Strengthening my marriage

With so much stress, how do we stay strong as a couple?

Sibling support

How do I make sure my typical child(ren) get what they need as they grow, too?

Navigating special education in the school system

What's the best way for me to interact with the school system? What can I expect from them in terms of services?

Finding friends for my child
What's the best ways for me to give my child the gift of having friends?

Understanding tears and tantrums
How should I respond to outbursts and aggressive behavior? What—if anything—can I do to prevent it?

Keeping transitions tranquil
How do I design experiences throughout the day so my child isn't upset by transitions?

Preparing my child to live in a world that doesn't always understand
What's the path toward giving my child the most independent, enjoyable future possible?

How to help without being a helicopter parent
When your child with special needs is so vulnerable, how can you help but hover?

My child is now an adult. What comes next?
How do I navigate adult resources like day support programs and housing options?

CHAPTER 24

NATIONAL RESPITE CARE ORGANIZATIONS WORTH KNOWING

*I*n the same way Jill's House benefited from a relationship with Shalva in Jerusalem, you can benefit from forming a relationship with Jill's House.

But there are other organizations worth knowing, too. Here are two favorites:

Joni & Friends

For 40 years, Joni & Friends has served individuals and families affected by disabilities and worked nationally and internationally to advance disability ministry.

In 1967, a 17-year-old Joni Eareckson suffered a diving accident that left her a quadriplegic in a wheelchair. Two years later, she left rehab with fresh skills and a single-minded determination to help others in similar situations.

In 1979, she founded Joni and Friends, which provides Jesus-centered programs to special needs families, churches, and communities.

Visit Joni & Friends' website, and you'll find links to a wide range of resources the organization makes available to churches like yours.

From hosting retreats to creating training materials to providing podcast, video, television, and radio programming, Joni & Friends is at the forefront of trumpeting the message that there's hope in Jesus for all people.

And if serving in respite care captures your heart like we think it will, it might be time to dust off your book bag and head back to class.

The Joni and Friends Christian Institute on Disability partners with universities and seminaries around the world to offer coursework designed to equip leaders for effective disability ministry.

Joni & Friends
(JoniandFriends.org)
(818) 707-5664

99 Balloons

This organization provides churches with tools for launching and maintaining a respite care ministry.[5]

"Our name reflects how many helium balloons were released at the funeral of Eliot Mooney—one for each day he was on earth," said 99 Balloons' Programs Director, Rebecca Wall.

Eliot's parents, Matt and Ginny Mooney, were told several months before their first child's due date that their baby had Edward's Syndrome.

The syndrome, a genetic disorder, is usually fatal. Affected babies often die before birth or survive only a few days following delivery. But that wasn't the case with Eliot.

On July 2, 2006, Eliot was greeted by parents determined to celebrate each day of his life with a birthday party, picture, and prayer of thanks.

Those parties lasted 99 days.

Then, as his parents wrote, "Our fighter of a son has gone to be with Jesus. We celebrate his life and revel in the fact that he is finally well."

Thankful for the outpouring of support and respite they received throughout Eliot's brief life, the Mooneys established 99 Balloons so other parents could have the same opportunity.

The Arkansas-based organization now provides training to churches of any size about how to build sustainable respite ministries.

"We provide training for church volunteers and also curriculum for monthly respite sessions," said Rebecca. "What churches find

---

5   https://www.everylifecounts.ie/stories/eliot-mooney

especially helpful is that there's not only a program of games, activities, crafts, and movies designed for children with disabilities, but we also provide curriculum for any typical siblings who come." 99 Balloons has helped launch nearly 50 church-based respite care programs in the U.S. and is also active in addressing special needs and respite care internationally.

"We're partnering with organizations in Haiti, Uganda, Nicaragua, and a location in Southern Asia," said Rebecca. "Our emphasis is training local teachers to include students with special needs, because 9 out of 10 children with disabilities in those locations don't currently attend school."

And when children with special needs attend school, good things happen.

Their mothers are able to find respite—and work—because their kids are cared for during school hours. The children are finally able to do what other kids do—have a community of friends, sit at a lunch table with peers, and prepare for their futures.

"When mothers can provide for their families, the cycle of poverty that often traps these families is broken," said Rebecca. "The ripple effect of moving children with disability out of the house and out into school is huge."

99 Balloons send teams annually to provide training to international partners, and the organization's "All-In Education" program lets individuals sponsor children and underwrite training for international teachers and therapists.

Like Jill's House, 99 Balloons welcomes calls from congregations wanting to create respite for families in their communities.

99 Balloons (99 Balloons.org)

And Don't Forget to Check with the Home Team...

If your church is part of a denomination, pick up the phone and call your denominational leadership.

Many denominations are eager to help member churches embrace special needs and respite ministries. You may find both training and funding waiting for you on the other end of the call.

CHAPTER 25

DEVOTIONS FOR STAFF AND VOLUNTEERS

*H*elp your volunteers see they're not just serving the special needs community—they're serving God, too. Jesus never failed to serve those with disabilities, and your volunteers can reflect that same acceptance and love.

But it takes more than just quality program and adequate training.

It's also a matter of the heart.

Ask your volunteers, as part of their training, to use the following daily devotions either during their first week of serving, or as part of each of their first seven times to serve (permission to copy these devotions granted by the publisher).

Remember that although many of these New Testament passages involve the miracle of healing, healing of disability isn't the focus of your ministry or the parents you will be serving. Healing can be a sensitive topic for parents who love their children exactly as they are.

A Heart of Compassion

A man with leprosy came and knelt in front of Jesus, begging to be healed. "If you are willing, you can heal me and make me clean," he said.

Moved with compassion, Jesus reached out and touched him. "I am willing," he said. "Be healed!"

Instantly the leprosy disappeared, and the man was healed.

(Mark 1:40-42)

IN JESUS' DAY, the leper who sought out Jesus was risking his life as he elbowed his way through the disciples to fall at the feet of Jesus.

Lepers were outcasts—living isolated lives far away from "normal" people. Their disabling disease often left them disfigured, prompting both fear and disgust from people they encountered.

Yet Jesus didn't see just a disease as he looked at the man crouched at his feet. Jesus' compassion saw past the disability to see the person, and Jesus reached out to touch that person to bring healing and wholeness.

As you serve families whose children have disabilities, your compassion brings far more hope than you know.

These families are accustomed to watching people look past their children. But you'll be leaning in, loving those children rather than looking away, giving hugs rather than awkward glances.

Your compassion brings help and hope.

God,

Give me a heart of compassion—help me see my own need for your healing touch.

Thank you for the special people I'll be serving. Help me see them as you see them—as people to love, not problems to solve.

Help me love others as you love me.

Amen.

A Heart to Help

One day while Jesus was teaching.... Some men came carrying a paralyzed man on a sleeping mat. They tried to take him inside to Jesus, but they couldn't reach him because of the crowd. So, they went up to the roof and took off some tiles. Then they lowered the sick man on his mat down into the crowd, right in front of Jesus.

Seeing their faith, Jesus said to the man, "Young man, your sins are forgiven."

Then Jesus turned to the paralyzed man and said, "Stand up, pick up your mat, and go home!"

And immediately, as everyone watched, the man jumped up, picked up his mat, and went home praising God."

(Luke 5:17-20, 24-25)

HERE'S THE THING about volunteering in respite care: You can't completely predict what's coming. No two days are the same.

So stay flexible. Do what's necessary, even if it pulls you outside your comfort zone. Even if it means climbing up on a roof and yanking off tiles.

Okay, that probably *won't* be something you do...but the paralyzed man's friends were willing to do it if it meant getting their buddy the help he needed.

As you serve, be constantly asking, "What will be helpful here? What else can I do?" That heart to help not only transforms the time you spend serving—it transforms you as well.

> *God,*
> *Give me a heart to help—one that asks, "What else can I do?"*
> *It's the heart you bring to our friendship, and I love that about you.*
> *Help that same heart be in me as I serve in respite care.*
> *Amen.*

A Heart of Respect

Afterward Jesus returned to Jerusalem for one of the Jewish holy days.
Inside the city, near the Sheep Gate, was the pool of Bethesda, with
five covered porches.
Crowds of sick people—blind, lame, or paralyzed—lay on the porches.
One of the men lying there had been sick for 38 years. When Jesus saw
him and knew he had been ill for a long time, he asked him, "Would
you like to get well?"
"I can't, sir," the sick man said, "for I have no one to put me into the pool
when the water bubbles up. Someone else always gets there ahead of me."
Jesus told him, "Stand up, pick up your mat, and walk!"
Instantly, the man was healed! He rolled up his sleeping mat and
began walking! But this miracle happened on the Sabbath...
(John 5:1-9)

THERE ARE TWO miracles tucked into this passage.

The first is Jesus healing a man whose legs refused to work for nearly
40 years. A man whose hope had withered as completely as his limbs.

And the second miracle is one of respect.

Jesus doesn't just heal the man: He asks if the man *wants* to be healed.
Jesus doesn't assume; he respectfully asks the man what he wants.

As we serve families with disabilities, it's easy to assume we know
what's best for the family, what will help their situation, and what they
should do or not do.

But we don't know. We haven't lived their lives or experienced what
they're experiencing. Even if we have a story of living with disabilities, our
story isn't their story. We don't truly know what they want or need.

So, ever and always, be respectful. Ask, rather than assume. Listen. Learn.
And love.

God,
Give me a heart of respect—for those with disabilities and their families.
Help me listen well. Learn quickly.
And love always.
Amen.

A Heart for Service

After washing their feet, he put on his robe again and sat down and asked, "Do you understand what I was doing?
"You call me 'Teacher' and 'Lord,' and you are right, because that's what I am.
"And since I, your Lord and Teacher, have washed your feet, you ought to wash each other's feet."
(John 13:12-14)

IN JESUS' DAY, nobody washed the dusty, sandaled feet of guests except servants or slaves. It certainly wasn't the role of a rabbi to kneel down and care for the feet of his followers.

Yet there Jesus is, leading by example.

The Kingdom of God is all *about* service. Jesus serves us in countless ways, including his death on the cross. He calls leaders to serve those they lead, followers to serve their leaders, and for all who follow him to serve one another.

So, as you embrace respite care, come to it as a servant.

Come to cheerfully meet the needs of children and their families.

Come willing to do what it takes—whatever it takes—to keep precious children safe and to help them feel loved and cherished.

Come not because of what you'll get, but what you'll give.

And here's a secret: If you come like that—if you come as a servant—you'll receive far more than you could ever imagine.

God,
Give me a heart to serve the children and families I meet in this ministry.
Help me set aside my pride and lower my walls.
You're my model, Jesus. Help me serve others like you serve me.
Thank you for this opportunity.
Let's do this together.
Amen.

A Heart for Rest

Then Jesus said, "Come to me, all of you who are weary and carry heavy burdens, and I will give you rest."
"Take my yoke upon you. Let me teach you, because I am humble and gentle at heart, and you will find rest for your souls.
"For my yoke is easy to bear, and the burden I give you is light."
(Matthew 11:28-30)

FAMILIES WITH SPECIAL needs children aren't likely to say they're carrying a light burden.

Many days are a blur of caregiving, doctor visits, meetings, and coping with an avalanche of paperwork. There's little time or margin for sleep, let alone exercise or investing in relationships.

All because they love someone.

It's easy to love people who so fiercely love their children. No wonder serving in respite care tugs at your heart even when you're away from your volunteer role.

But do this: Get rest so you can help others have rest. Pace yourself—because the people you serve often aren't able to pace themselves.

It's not selfish to take care of yourself so you can care for others. It's exactly like that warning you receive when you board an airplane: In the unlikely event of a sudden drop in pressure, put on your own oxygen mask before assisting others.

So, rest...and ask God for opportunities to talk with the families you serve about the ultimate source of rejuvenating rest: Jesus.

God,
Thank you for inventing rest—what a gift to your frantic creations.
Help me experience rest in you so I can share that restoring rest with others.
Thank you for making yourself known in the thunder of storms and the calm of a quiet morning. In booming action...and quiet rest.
Help us all to rest in you, God.
Amen.

A Heart to See People, Not Problems

The LORD doesn't see things the way you see them. People judge by outward appearance, but the LORD looks at the heart.
(1 Samuel 16:7)

WHEN SAMUEL WAS scouting around for Israel's next king, he didn't put David anywhere close to the top of the list.

Because, frankly, the kid had a few problems.

He was short, young, and a shepherd. That's three strikes when you're selecting potential royalty, and it took God speaking to Samuel to prompt the prophet to look past the obvious to what God was seeing in his heart.

As you serve children and their families in respite care, you'll see a lot of "shortcomings," like exhausted parents and kids who may be different—but there's more than meets the eye.

Consider how desperately these parents love their children, and their children love them. How quickly you're accepted by children who choose to embrace their world by leading with love. And how honored you feel to be trusted to care for these kids.

Then read the passage above again.

You're living the lesson Samuel learned. What a blessing!

God,
You're so quick to love me—and others, too.
Give me your eyes to see children with disabilities for who they are.
Thank you for the majesty you've crafted into your creations—all of your creations.
You do great work, God.
Amen.

A Heart of Gratitude

Don't worry about anything; instead, pray about everything.
Tell God what you need, and thank him for all he has done.
(Philippians 4:6)

WHEN YOU SERVE in respite care, it's hard to avoid feeling grateful.

You're hanging out with some of the most remarkable people on the planet. With parents who go the second mile as a sort of warm-up lap. With children who look beyond their discomfort and disabilities to see you and smile.

You begin catching a glimpse of who God has made you to be.

Someone with love to share.

Someone with a strength that stretches further than you thought possible.

Someone with a heart tuned to gratitude.

You're better for rubbing shoulders with families with disabilities. You're kinder, more aware, and more thankful for the blessing they are in your life.

So, thank them sometime for what they bring to your life—it may be the first time anyone has ever paused to say the words.

God,
Thank you for the people I serve in respite care.
Thank you that you allow me to serve in this way.
You're making me a better person because of this experience—and I'm
grateful for that.
For that, and so much more.
Amen.

ADA Checklist

The following checklist will give you a good idea whether a space will work for respite care.

Accessibility begins outside your building...

❑ Can you get from the parking lot inside to your respite area without encountering steps or curbs?

❑ Are accessible entrances clearly marked?

❑ Are there clearly-marked handicap parking spots available? A designated drop-off spot?

❑ Does the slope of the sidewalk exceed a 5% rise?

❑ Do concrete slabs have a curved cut?

❑ Is the closest door wheelchair accessible, with a level platform that's a minimum of five square feet if the door swings outward?

❑ Do doors have a minimum of a 36" opening when opened?

❑ Can doors be opened to get to 36" in one easy motion as opposed to having to open two doors at once?

❑ Have doors been automated to open with a push button?

❑ Are there any bumps or abrupt differences in floor levels by door sills?

Once through the doors...

☐ Are all hallways at least 36" wide?

☐ Are there acceptably inclined ramps connecting all rooms?

☐ Are ramp inclines on a slope that's a rise of one foot in 12 feet?

☐ Do ramps have handrails on both sides?

☐ Is the height of those handrails consistently 36" from the ramp surface?

☐ Do handrails extend at least 12 inches past each ramp's top and bottom?

☐ Are handrails smooth and the proper diameter?

☐ Are tabletops used for activities at a height easily reached by those in wheelchairs?

☐ Are all interior routes and spaces free of obstructions?

☐ Is there an accessible water fountain on each floor?

☐ Are all signs used to identify rooms installed on the wall adjacent to the latch side of the door on the nearest adjacent wall?

☐ Are signs 60 inches from the floor?

☐ Are important signs in Braille?

☐ If you'll use rooms on multiple floors, do you have an accessible elevator?

☐ Do alarm lights flash as well as emit sound?

☐ Are you ready to deal with service animals?

☐ Is carpet smooth rather than plush?

And because nature calls...

❑ Is there at least one accessible restroom available on every floor used for respite?

❑ In restrooms is there a stall that's at least 36 inches wide?

❑ Does the accessible stall have a turning space of at least five square feet?

❑ From the door of the stall to the toilet is there a distance of at least 48 inches?

❑ Is the stall door at least 36 inches wide?

❑ Is the toilet seat between 17 and 19 inches from the floor?

❑ Are grab bars installed as recommended in ADA regulations?

❑ Are there lever handles on hardware?

❑ Are sinks and towel dispensers accessible?

❑ Are mirrors above sink only or are they full-length mirrors?